THE
MASCULINE JOURNEY

UNDERSTANDING THE
SIX STAGES OF MANHOOD

A Promise Keepers Study Guide

ROBERT HICKS WITH DIETRICH GRUEN

NAVPRESS

BRINGING TRUTH TO LIFE
NavPress Publishing Group
P.O. Box 35001, Colorado Springs, Colorado 80935

The Navigators is an international Christian organization. Jesus Christ gave His followers the Great Commission to go and make disciples (Matthew 28:19). The aim of The Navigators is to help fulfill that commission by multiplying laborers for Christ in every nation.

NavPress is the publishing ministry of The Navigators. NavPress publications are tools to help Christians grow. Although publications alone cannot make disciples or change lives, they can help believers learn biblical discipleship, and apply what they learn to their lives and ministries.

Second printing, 1993

Some of the anecdotal illustrations in this book are true to life and are included with the permission of the persons involved. All other illustrations are composites of real situations, and any resemblance to people living or dead is coincidental.

Unless otherwise identified, all Scripture quotations in this publication are taken from the *New American Standard Bible* (NASB), © The Lockman Foundation 1960, 1962, 1963, 1968, 1971, 1972, 1973, 1975, 1977. Other versions used include: the *HOLY BIBLE: NEW INTERNATIONAL VERSION*® (NIV®), Copyright © 1973, 1978, 1984 by International Bible Society, used by permission of Zondervan Publishing House, all rights reserved.

Printed in the United States of America

FOR A FREE CATALOG OF
NAVPRESS BOOKS & BIBLE STUDIES,
CALL 1-800-366-7788 (USA)
or 1-416-499-4615 (CANADA)

Contents

◆

How to Use This Guide

♦

What does it mean to be a man? Part of the reason it's hard to answer this question is that manhood is not static. It's a journey. The book *The Masculine Journey* explores six key elements of the process of being a man. This discussion guide is a companion to that book. It will introduce you to some of the central ideas of the book and give you a chance to discuss and practice them. You don't have to read the book in order to use this guide because each discussion session includes an excerpt from the book. However, this guide only scratches the surface of each concept, so you may find yourself wanting to delve into the book for further explanation and examples.

Because most of us have busy schedules, this guide is designed so that as participants you don't have to prepare anything in advance of your discussion sessions. Instead, each session includes some ideas for taking home what you've learned and putting it into practice. During the discussions, you can jot your thoughts and responses in this guide.

Each session contains the following sections:

Identifying the Issues with Robert Hicks. This material is excerpted and adapted from the book *The Masculine Journey.* Someone in the group can read this aloud, or you can take a few minutes to read it silently. Each session tells you where to go in the book to read more about that session's subject.

Exploring the Issues with Other Men. The questions in this section will help you discuss what you've read. You'll compare your own experiences with what Robert Hicks says.

5

Profiling a Bible Character. In his book, Hicks uses a different biblical character as an example of each facet of manhood. This section will give you a chance to look at some of the biblical stories about those men and see for yourself what you think.

Bringing It Home to Yourself and Other Men. In this section you'll consider what you might do about what you've been discussing.

Taking It Further with Other Studies. If you're interested in learning more about the topic of a session, this section gives several options for further biblical study.

If you are the group leader, be sure to read the "Help for Leaders" section, beginning on page 91.

An Uneasy
Men's Movement

◆

IDENTIFYING THE ISSUES WITH ROBERT HICKS
Excerpted and adapted from *The Masculine Journey*, pages 13-28.

I hate maps. They take all the challenge out of life. So I try to do it on my own, and I get lost. The masculine experience is like that. Whether as developing teenagers, midlife males, or senior mentors, men need a kind of map that shows us what's up ahead, and how we are to get from one point to another.

Not All Is Well with Men
In a sense, this book is a sequel to *Uneasy Manhood*, my previous work on men's issues. Since the publication of that first book, much has happened in the men's movement. Men are openly reading and discussing new male topics to rediscover something that they feel has been lost. For most men all the discussion about the "fire in the belly," the "wild man within us," "primitive archetypes," and "primary fantasies" is fairly high sounding and theoretical. What men want to know is, "What does it mean to be a man?"

In *Uneasy Manhood*, my goal was to explore the areas of uneasiness among men. I worked on the premise that all was not well with men in our American society. However, on the talk-show circuit one has to interact face to face with one's audience. On one nationwide program, the host asked me, "So what is a man?" I didn't have a clue! I saw myself backpedaling, quoting other writers, avoiding any statement that our feminist-aware culture might view as not "politically correct."

7

What Is a Man?
The question is fundamentally simple; the answer, elusive. I wasn't satisfied with most "expert" definitions.

The pre-feminist 1950s saw the real man as John Wayne, the strong-quiet type. The postfeminist era placed more emphasis on the Alan Alda type, the sensitive-nurturing male. More recently Sly Stallone, Arnold Schwarzenegger, Norman Schwarzkopf, and Ross Perot illustrate the way men ought to be.

The options are many. Is the true man one who has found his feminine side, or his wild man? Is he the strong male, the sensitive male, or the successful-in-business male? Or is true manhood just plain celluloid that doesn't really exist anywhere except in our fantasies?

"What is a man?" The question continued to roll over in my mind. Then I remembered Daniel Levinson's *The Seasons of a Man's Life*. Levinson draws a developmental framework for understanding men: Manhood is reflected differently in certain predictable eras throughout the adult life cycle.

The Developmental Journey
Adult life is not static, but a journey where the landscape is constantly changing. Every new encounter demands some appropriate response or adjustment. What defines a man in his twenties is not the same as what may characterize a man in his forties.

Understanding the male experience as a journey suggests times of *separation* from the past, *initiation* to something new, *transition* from one place to the other, and temporary *confusion*. Some developmental tasks such as marriage are very intentional and predictable. At times, such as job loss, adjustment and transition may be harder and longer, but the experience just the same is normative for a man.

Six Words from Hebrew 101: The Stages of the Journey
I believe there *is* a normative male. As a biblically trained theologian I asked, "Does Scripture have anything to contribute in this regard?" Six words for "man," learned in Hebrew class years earlier, now shed the light I needed. This biblical framework described the long-standing male experience throughout the centuries and was true to the current literature. The words also seem to reflect the same seasonal or developmental aspects that have been demonstrated in recent men's studies.

The Masculine Journey draws from these six Hebrew words to create concepts about the male experience. The meaning I ascribe to these six words is not exclusive. However, as I use the words, they say something very descriptive and normative about the masculine experience, which in turn, helps map the meaning of manhood.

What triggered this Hebrew word approach was a familiar proverb: "The glory of young men is their strength, and the honor of old men is their gray hair" (20:29). The implications: *What a man is depends on what season he is in*—that is, what station he has reached on the journey of manhood. Young men are defined by their warrior strength, old men by their wisdom. Children need to know their sins are forgiven, younger men need to overcome their tendency to do evil, and older men must continue their spiritual persistence (1 John 2:12-14).

The foundational Hebrew word for man, *'adam*, can refer to either male or female. This first experience of maleness mapped out in Scripture is the only one shared with our feminine counterparts. It reflects the generic idea that men and women are *creational* beings first and foremost. We are not derived from ourselves nor do we live exclusively for ourselves, but we ultimately must reflect our Creator. As creational males we are flesh and blood, material beings who will one day return to dust. Being creational means we have unique capabilities that are honorable and divine, but which can be used for evil.

The second Hebrew word, *zakar*, reflects the *phallic male* in his distinct sexual aspect. Men, as phallic beings, have an innate sexual focus, which has been denied, denigrated, or perverted in our culture. Some men are very phallic-aware but have fixated at the phallic stage of development, even men in their fifties and sixties. They have never grown up and moved on in their maleness.

The Hebrew word *gibbor* reflects the male in his warring strength. Young adult men war on the athletic fields, war in their minds in graduate schools, war in business, war in Southeast and Southwest Asia. As with phallic man, the warrior has been devalued in our society but is often over-glorified. He is the honored hero. However, warriors get wounded.

The fourth Hebrew word for man is *enosh*, which describes man in his weakness, in his frailty, and in his woundedness. He has been wounded by various "swords": by abusive and absent fathers; by domineering mothers and teachers; by the

9

educational system; by toxic takeovers in business; by layoffs; by failure, by success; by alcohol; by divorce; by his own friend-lessness; by poverty, by wealth. No matter what brought the sword to his heart, the warrior is now wounded and bleeding. The "wounded male" has been called the masculine metaphor for the nineties.

The most common American male image of manhood is probably the solitary man on horseback, who knows exactly what he is all about and who has said no to many other voices in his life.

The fifth Hebrew term *'ish* reflects this differentiated male ruling over his own spirit. He is his own man—he knows who he really is and what he is all about, apart from anyone else. The ruling male is thus "attributal," in that he is usually characterized by his own attributes. He is also known by his relationships, especially with women. A man cannot become the ruler of his own soul and genuine in his relationships until he has been through some wounding. He can then begin to listen to the voice of God more clearly, and to the leanings of his own conscience and values. Some men do it, many don't. For those who don't, life stagnates. For the man who starts to rule his own soul, life gets more exciting and leads to his greatest contributions and achievements.

The last word is *zaken*, the Hebrew word for elder. It is the last stop on the masculine journey. The word literally means "gray-headed," reflecting the idea of the wise mentor or sage. The Bible sees this man connected to all of life, making his most important contributions to the community and culture. He also mentors the younger men. Our sages today have either been scorned into hiding or they don't exist. It's time we find them and put them to work. The *zaken* time of life is the destination on the journey, so let's celebrate it.

EXPLORING THE ISSUES WITH OTHER MEN

1. Men are openly reading and discussing new male topics in an attempt to rediscover something they feel has been lost. Which of the following authors and/or topics are you familiar with?

   ❑ Sam Keen encouraged us to find the "fire in the belly" (renewed with heart on-fire, zealous for issues

10

close to hearth and big as the earth).
- ❑ Robert Bly wants us to find the "wild man within," who lives in the forest of our lives and will mentor the young boy in search of his manhood.
- ❑ Robert Johnson puts us on a search for the lost feminine.
- ❑ Sam Osherson advises us to reconnect with our lost fathers.
- ❑ Deborah Tannen tell us that we speak and hear very different languages from women.
- ❑ Warren Farrell reveals that, despite all the talk about the gender social revolution, both men and women have remained firmly rooted to their primary fantasies.

2. What do you feel is not well with men? Or, what do you hope to find in this study for yourself?

3. Imagine yourself as Robert Hicks before he wrote this book. You are the one token male on that nationally syndicated talk show. Then you are thrust back on your heels with the haunting question from the female host: What is a man? How would you reply? You may fall back on any outside reading you have done, but do not refer to *The Masculine Journey*.

4. a. Which made-for-TV role models of manhood were you raised with? Of these and others, which do you admire or resemble most?

   ❑ John Wayne
   ❑ Bill Cosby
   ❑ Michael Gross (in "Family Ties")
   ❑ Fred McMurray (in "My Three Sons")
   ❑ Robert Reed (in "The Brady Bunch")
   ❑ "Bonanza" — which character?

❑ "M*A*S*H" — which character?
❑ "The Waltons" — which character?
❑ "Father Knows Best" — which character?
❑ "Leave It to Beaver" — which character?
❑ Other:

b. Which real-life father figures, or older male mentors, have shown you what a "real man" is?

5. In the absence of true fathers and older male mentors in our culture, and with the dominance of feminist definitions and "politically correct" expectations about maleness, Robert Hicks dares to talk about the normative masculine experience. What is your reaction to this?

❑ In the area of gender, nothing is normative anymore.
❑ Normative is whatever one grew up or experienced along the way.
❑ Normative is whatever the Bible says.
❑ Normative is whatever cultural stereotypes prevail — on television.
❑ Science has discovered critical differences between men and women.
❑ Other:

6. a. What is your church doing to make up for the present lack of true fathers and older male mentors?

b. What expectations do you have that this book, or the men in your study group, will help in that regard?

PROFILING A BIBLE CHARACTER

In each session we will trace one of the six male traits through the lives of classic Bible characters. In this first session, however, we merely introduce the main concepts to you. Even so, certain Bible characters may come to mind that epitomize certain of these male traits.

7. If the six Hebrew words defining maleness sound familiar to you, perhaps you are either a Hebrew scholar or you have been reading about these concepts in sources outside the Bible.

   a. From whatever source, which of the six concepts is most familiar to you?

   b. Which are descriptive of the men you know best?

   c. Which male concepts raise nagging or haunting questions for you?

8. In the chart below, define or describe each of the six Hebrew terms in your own words. Next, think about Bible characters who might fit each description. Try to match at least one Bible character with each male character trait. (*Hint:* These twelve Bible characters will match up with the six male traits that Hicks identified: Abraham, Jacob, Samson, David, Joab, Solomon, Elijah,

Job, Jeremiah, Jesus Christ, Barnabas, and Paul.) Compare answers among your group. You'll find that Bible characters, as with anybody, exhibit more than one developmental trait or stage.

HEBREW WORD	DEFINITION	BIBLE CHARACTER
'Adam		
Zakar		
Gibbor		
Enosh		
'Ish		
Zaken		

BRINGING IT HOME TO YOURSELF AND OTHER MEN

The purpose of this section is to apply the principles we've studied, and to do so within the safety and confidence of fellow strugglers. In future sessions these questions are designed to translate truth into action. This week the exercise is designed to help get your men into a group.

> **Note to the leader:** Set a time limit and additional rules appropriate to your size group for the following game. For example, limit large groups (over sixteen in number) to one signature per box on the scorecard. You might suggest that everyone use pencils so you can erase the scorecard later and play the game again with another group of men.

9. People Bingo: The object of this game is to meet as many different men in your group as possible, to get a handle on them, and to establish some points of commonality. Review the categories in the scorecard or grid below. Walk around your group and try to find men who fit a category or have that trait or experience. When you meet someone who fits the description, he can initial the appropriate box on your scorecard. More than one person can fill in any given box, and the same person might suit more than one box. The first person to complete five in a row—column or diagonal—within the set time limit wins. Competition should bring out the warrior in each man!

> **Note to the leader:** Stop "People Bingo" when appropriate, even if there is no declared winner. The winners are all those who enjoyed getting to know the masculine experience of others. Not coincidentally, this exercise introduced the group, in a fun way, to several of the not-always-fun masculine experiences to be explored in *The Masculine Journey*. Spend time debriefing, perhaps by asking for the answers to certain categories, or by asking participants to identify which boxes had their name. Do whatever you have time for, perhaps over refreshments. Allow men who are uneasy about their male journey to express this.

Is wearing boxer shorts *or* bikini briefs	Plays golf or tennis competitively	Has a sister active in the feminist movement	Has coached his son's soccer or baseball team	Has had circumcision, vasectomy, *or* prostate operation
Has been arrested at least once	Has emotional battle scars from a recent family feud	Works out often to keep in shape	Is a supervisor at work or an elder at church	Has a father who invested lots of time in him
Was neglected or abused by father	Has made most of his funeral arrangements	Suffered through a divorce or death of spouse	Broke off an engagement to be married	Is very creative in arts and crafts
Has been laid off from work recently	Never needs to consult a map	Has suffered a recent injury or ill health	Is the oldest male in the group	Has said "I'll quit tomorrow," but didn't
Has read two books on men's movement	Won a company sales competition	Is going through a mid-life crisis	Resembles the Marlboro Man	Has a tattoo or war wound (and can show it)

The six main stops on the masculine journey will be further explored, one at a time, in the next six sessions. Make a commitment among yourselves to support the other men on this new male journey. Read chapter 2 in *The Masculine Journey*—if you have not already done so, read chapter 1. As we look at the *creational male*, or noble savage, ponder these quotes:

> Man with all his noble qualities still bears in his bodily frame the indelible stamp of his lowly origin.
> —Charles Darwin, from *The Descent of Man*

> Do impulses toward sadistic cruelty lurk in the depths of every human psyche?
> —Anthony Storr, from *Human Destructiveness*

In preparation for the next session, begin thinking how you are like, and unlike, men from so-called "primitive societies."

Creational Male—
'Adam: The Noble Savage

◆

IDENTIFYING THE ISSUES WITH ROBERT HICKS
Excerpted and adapted from *The Masculine Journey*, pages 31-43.

Within every upward desire, there is a countering downward pull. Within the most noble of desires there also exists an often surprising savagery. To cite Margaret Mead's often-used term for the uncivilized people groups she studied, we as men (and all humankind) are *noble savages*.

The first stage on the masculine journey is the only one that includes our female counterparts. The other five words will focus on how men experience their humanness—in contrast to women—on the different points on the masculine journey. The usage of *'adam* reveals four ideas about what it means to be a creational kind of guy.

Created for Relationships
To be creational males means to realize we as men have not been created for ourselves. We owe something back to God. We are not created and given life to go our merry way without so much as a "thank You."

We are God's representatives on earth. Having a relationship with the living God also means that in this ruling function we as men must form a certain benevolent relationship with the earth and our fellowmen. The rulership envisioned in Genesis 1:28 implies the rule of wisdom, care, and stewardship of God's territory. This accountability is extended to those living on the earth. The issues of justice, kindness, and humility before God are placed on 'adam (Micah 6:8, Romans 12:14-20, Galatians 6:10).

As men we can try to run away from our Creator and our God-given responsibilities, but we must realize that we are running away from not only ourselves but also from what it means to be manly. I have known men who were unconsciously running from God for years to pursue other passions. But when these men finally understand Christianity as a personal relationship with Christ and see His masculinity, they respond differently. I believe all men are "Christ-haunted" and hunted down, until they truly see what it is they are rejecting. When they realize they have been running from a mere caricature of Christianity, they fall down in tears and see the One for whom they were made. The Bible calls this repentance; I call it being manly! Without accepting the creaturely realities of being made by and for our heavenly Father, we cannot be the men we should.

'Adam also reveals man in his relations with women, the feminine counterpart (Genesis 2:18-25). This is more than the usual explanation that "opposites attract." God created the sexes as opposites, giving a mystical and magical quality to the relationship. As men, when we look into the mirror after showering and see our unique sexual equipment it is a reminder that we are made for another.

Created with Dignity

It seems the entire self-help movement has assumed that self-esteem is something to be valued, sought, and recovered. As a Christian, I wonder how writers who have no theological or philosophical orientation can assume such a massive first premise. Why should the *self* be something that should be valued and improved? As I understand modern psychological literature, there is very little explanation as to why this first assumption exists. Whereas, if God has made both male and female in His own image, there is something to be valued and esteemed in the self of every human being. If humans have no special creational worth, then why not blow them away, or treat them inhumanely?

To be creaturely means to have a dignity and worth not derived from our performance or achievements but by our birth and being. As men, we have value because we merely *are*, not because of what we *do* or accomplish. I can lose my job, my

19

marriage, my kids, and suffer the loss of self-esteem, but this does not mean I have none. I know few men who have this reality so deeply rooted in their psyches that they never suffer from the performance syndrome. But at least it is encouraging to know I have value for no other reason than just being.

When I have been disgraced by events or circumstances, I fight to regain some sense of dignity. This struggle for dignity (wrongly called pride) reveals only who and what I really am—a creational male. The therapeutic remedies and the self-help literature that are designed to recover or develop self-esteem only affirm this intrinsic, deeply rooted but unexplained value. Our value is explainable only by creation and a Creator!

Creational Mortality

The original dignity with which God made man did not last long. Apparently, had 'adam not sinned, he could have continued to eat at the tree of life and been immortal (Genesis 2:17, 3:22-24). The reality men often deny or pretend doesn't affect them is this foreboding sense of mortality. We think we will live forever—that we won't have heart attacks, lose our capabilities, our health, or our minds.

Eventually, we as men must face the fact that we will die and turn back to dust (Numbers 16:29, Psalm 90:3). Such tombstone theology is rarely taught in seminaries or churches, and the cosmetic, health, and exercise industries would like us to think otherwise. Wherever youthful sexuality and physical appearance are worshiped, there is rampant denial of mortality and the final reality that we will age, decline, and face the deterioration of our minds, bodies, and spirits.

Life always promises more than it can deliver, and the result is a sense of mortal uneasiness and emptiness. It usually takes the loss of job, marriage, or health for this reality to become a part of our personal conscience and convictions. Facing the mortality of life and finally figuring out that life is beyond our comprehension (as the author of Ecclesiastes did) is not easy. But it is a necessary part of the male experience.

Creational Savagery

When Margaret Mead first started studying the primitive peoples of Polynesia and Micronesia, she did not encounter the savagery often portrayed by Western writers and missionaries, instead she found unexpected and unexplainable nobility. Today, with all the emphasis on high aspirations in "civilized countries," the real question is how to explain the surprising amount and extent of violence, greed, and human degradation. Underneath the veneer of noble culture, we find horrific evil. The person in the appearance of a saint is a savage! How can this be?

The savagery of the soul should not surprise us. Being made in God's image, we possess great capabilities for good, but creational beings also have the freedom to pursue unholy courses and to become the most evil of men. We all carry airbrushed portraits of ourselves that show no blemishes or scars. But historical realities, such as the Holocaust, stand as stark reminders of who we really are as humans. On many occasions I have "compartmentalized" in my mind in order to carry out someone else's unjust wishes. The difference is the degree and the job description. The psychology is the same.

Until I realize the evil that I am capable of, I don't really believe that Jesus Christ means all that much. I may know I am saved, but have no real idea of what I am saved from.

As men, we naively think that the world is divided into two groups of people—good and bad. We, of course, are the good guys. But this is both psychological lunacy and theological madness. Remember Ecclesiastes: We have vanity, even *insanity*, in our hearts.

EXPLORING THE ISSUES WITH OTHER MEN

1. Many men grow up with models of masculinity (from their fathers, grandfathers, uncles, teachers, coaches) that they then project on to Christ. What were your male models like as you were growing up, and how did Jesus compare as a man?

   ❑ Both Jesus and the men I knew were meek and mild lovers of children.
   ❑ Both could be seen at lakeside hanging around fishermen.
   ❑ Both were wise and good teachers.
   ❑ Both were regular guys, sexually tempted as men are.
   ❑ Both were wounded healers, betrayed and bruised by/for our sin.

21

❑ Dad was a passive wimp, but not Jesus, who cracked a whip.
❑ Dad was an old cuss and Jesus was just another swear word.
❑ Other:

2. Hicks counters the prevailing notion that repentance is for wimps, or that Christianity is for losers, by showing how "repentance" is indeed the only "manly" thing to do when haunted by Christ.

   a. When did you first become aware that you were created for a relationship with the heavenly Father?

   b. Was there a time when you were especially "Christ-haunted"? Explain.

   c. What difference do you see, if any, between "repentance" and "being manly"?

   d. If not at times of repentance, then when have you felt most manly?

3. a. Many men get trapped in the "performance syndrome," which values a man for what he can produce. By contrast, Christianity places a high value on men for no other reason than just being. What gives you your greatest sense of worth and dignity? Be honest.

   ❑ What people say about me.
   ❑ What I accomplished in "my glory days."
   ❑ My monthly paycheck or my financial net worth.

❏ God's love letters to me in Scripture.
❏ Other:

b. What word picture describes the way you feel when you are convinced you have great worth and dignity? Draw or describe that picture.

4. The text of *The Masculine Journey* points out many painful ways that life leaves us with a sense of mortal uneasiness and emptiness.

   a. When has life struck a blow that confronted you with your own mortality, so that the fragility of life became a part of your everyday conscience or convictions?

   b. What have you done to prepare for your own inevitable death?

5. a. When you look in the mirror, do you see a *saint* or a *savage*?

   ❏ Depends on how recently I've shaved or what shape my body is in.
   ❏ Depends on who is the basis of comparison—primitives or moderns.
   ❏ I look better, even saintly, compared to 90 percent of the men my age.
   ❏ I see a savage when I look inside at my primitive

instincts and the hatred or horrible things I am
capable of.
❑ Other:

b. How do you account for both the savagery and the
nobility of man?

❑ My family tree has a lot to do with it.
❑ Original sin had something to do with it.
❑ I work to keep my nose clean; I'm a basically good
guy.
❑ I see a poor reflection of my evil, as in a darkened
mirror.
❑ Other:

PROFILING A BIBLE CHARACTER

Solomon, the third king in Israel's history, embodies both
creational greatness and extreme sinfulness. Hence we profile
him as the noble savage. Read 1 Kings 3:4-28, 10:23-11:6, and
Ecclesiastes 2.

6. Solomon was the *'adam* kind of man at his highest—creational, serving, caring, generative for good. What stories
recorded in Scripture portray these noble aspects of King
Solomon?

7. Solomon was a student of the aspirations and expectations of life, and he reached the conclusion that man's
mortality and ultimate destiny was futility. What rude
experiences in Solomon's life might have contributed to
this desperate conclusion? (See Ecclesiastes 2.)

This king who started out pleasing God and saving lives ended up serving his own pleasures and passions apart from God (1 Kings 3, 11). Robert Hicks comments on that tragic turn of events and dual nature of the king.

Solomon built a house for God, but he built an even bigger house for himself (compare 1 Kings 6 and 7). He loved foreign women and had over 700 wives, many of whom turned his heart away from the Lord (1 Kings 11:1-13). Solomon had no problem in raising a first-class army—he used foreign legions and forced labor from those he defeated. All this was in direct opposition to the decree that kings not multiply horses, wives, or wealth (Deuteronomy 17:16-17).

In other words, Solomon was not only a noble, spiritually minded monarch, but also a man of lower nature debauchery. He loved women, wealth, and the power his reign brought him. Solomon was a sinner. His abilities were used for good and evil. The legacy he left was a symbol of his divided heart. His two sons, after his death, split the kingdom in two, which remained divided throughout the rest of Israel's history. (*Excerpted and adapted from* The Masculine Journey, *pages 44-45.*)

8. Using this story as a mirror for your own life, what do you see? At what points do you see your noble nature reflected? Where do you see the savage?

9. The noble and the savage aspects of Solomon's character, role, and behavior are manifest in many contemporary figures active in politics, athletics, religion, and our everyday lives. What of Solomon's mixed message do you see in well-known people today?

10. We are blind to, or shielded from, the reality of our own evil, even though daily news of violence, greed, and degradation confront us with evidence to support the biblical doctrine that every part of us is tainted. What is your reaction when you see or read about the maniacal serial killer . . . the child molester . . . the Wall Street scam artist . . . or the power-hungry hedonist who finally falls from spiritual leadership?

 ❑ I agree with Alexander Solzhenitsyn: "The line that divides good and evil is not a line that divides good men from bad men, but a line which cuts through the middle of every human heart."
 ❑ I scoff at such news: "I'd never do that"; "I'm glad I don't have to deal with that evil"; or "Thank God that only happens there, not here."
 ❑ "There, but for the grace of God, go I."
 ❑ Other:

11. With yourself, with God, and with one other person, review what is in your heart and make a confession of any evil thoughts or potential for immoral deeds that may still be harbored there.

 Having confessed your own sinfulness before God and one other person, recreate in your mind's eye the word picture that described the way you felt when you were convinced you had great worth and dignity (see question 3).

 a. Do you still feel the same when you realize what evil you are capable of? Or do you feel valued only when doing something good or worthwhile? Explain. (Only God's radical grace can free us from thinking that it's what we do, not who we are, that matters most to God.)

b. Read Romans 5:6-9. How does the death of Christ relate to the *noble savage,* or creational male, which is each of us? Take a moment to thank God for sending Jesus to "die for the ungodly" — even you.

This first stop on the masculine journey we share in common with all humankind — male and female. The next step takes us to a distinctly male fork in the road. Read chapter 3 in *The Masculine Journey* to prepare for the next session. As we look at the phallic male, ponder these quotes:

> The passions should be held in reverence.
> — Edgar Allen Poe, from "The Raven"

> The loins are the place of judgment.
> — N. O. Brown, quoted in *Fire in the Belly*

In preparation for the next session, begin thinking through the differences that distinguish male and female sexuality. The current debate over equality of the sexes, sexual orientation, and gender discrimination tends to blur the very real differences — physical and emotional, inherent and acquired, biblical and cultural — between male and female.

TAKING IT FURTHER WITH OTHER STUDIES

- ◆ On man's creational dignity and worth: Genesis 1; Psalm 8, 85:10-13, 139:13-16; Isaiah 43:1-7
- ◆ On the reality of evil: Genesis 6:1-5; Psalm 38, 51, 78:1-22; Proverbs 1; Isaiah 54:11-17; Ezekiel 20, 28:12-19; Romans 1:18-32; 1 Timothy 6:6-10
- ◆ On human frailty and mortality: Job 3, 14, 25; Psalm 49:10-19, 78:32-42
- ◆ Other Bible characters who embody themes of this session are Moses (Exodus 2-4), Hezekiah (2 Kings 16:20–20:21), and Jonah.

The Phallic Male—
Zakar: The Mysterious
Taskmaster

◆

IDENTIFYING THE ISSUES WITH ROBERT HICKS
Excerpted and adapted from *The Masculine Journey*, pages 47-66.

Maleness and femaleness has become something to be debated and politicized. This is where the ancient wisdom of the Bible provides additional help in acting as a map for our masculine experience.

The Phallus as the Organ of Gender Discrimination
The Hebrew word *zakar*, which is usually translated as "male" in distinction to female has to do with the male protrusion, hence the male penis or phallus. The Scriptures root male identity and sexuality firmly in anatomy, rather than in psychology or sociology. I am a male, whether I feel like it or not, whether or not I ever do anything considered masculine by the culture in which I live. This is the fixed point on the masculine journey, grounding my identity as a man in something that will never change.

The Phallus to Determine Religious Service
Spiritual service in the Old Testament was regulated by gender. Animal offerings during Israel's feasts were made on the basis of gender (Leviticus 3:1,6; 5:6; 22:19), yet only the male was required to bring a sacrifice (Exodus 23:17, 34:23). Only males were counted in the national census, and only males could be priests (Numbers 1:2,20,22; Leviticus 8:1). In certain wars all males were killed, while women and children were allowed to live (Deuteronomy 20:13-14). Men also got

to pay far more money than women for making the same vows (Leviticus 27:3-6).

There is no conflict between sexuality and spirituality. We are called to worship God in accordance with what we are: phallic men; not androgynous, neutered nonmales, or the feminized males so popular in "enlightened churches."

The Phallus as the Symbol of Dedication and Connection

The phallus is singled out as the unique site for the first wound and bloodletting a man will face—circumcision (Genesis 17:10,14). Removing the foreskin from the penis was a sign of both the male child's dedication to God and his being linked to the community of Israel. Circumcision symbolized God's faithfulness in providing male offspring who could reproduce more offspring to continue the covenant. In this sense, man's sexuality took on spiritual significance. Every use of his penis was making a spiritual statement about who he was and who he worshiped and why. It always does in every culture!

In modern culture the phallus has been separated from spiritual categories. In some religious circles the phallus has been viewed as a spiritual liability, barring women from the priesthood or diverting a man's attention from spiritual things. The church has been reacting and overreacting on the relation of sexuality to spirituality ever since Paul wrote 1 Corinthians 6–7 to correct misunderstandings in the early church.

A scriptural theology of sexuality joins spiritual and sexual issues properly. Until the church sees men for what they are—phallic males with all their inherent spiritual tensions—it will not begin to reach men where they are living. Without proper teaching on the phallus, men will carry around in their psyches a spiritual God-hunger so mysterious and powerful that, when driven underground, it will seek spiritual fulfillment in topless nightclubs, endless affairs, gay bars, adult videos, and locker room bragging.

Our sexual problems reveal only how desperate we are to express, in some perverted form, the deep compulsion to worship with our phallus. Many men get stuck in Phallic City, though it is a normal part of a developing manhood. When the phallus is given over to its full-blown spiritual power without restraint, it becomes an idol. Therefore, God regulates the use of the phallus, lest it become a very mysterious taskmaster.

The Phallus in Regulation

For Israel's survival as a nation and for their own good God gave them regulations and ordinances (Leviticus 18:5, Deuteronomy 6:24). Like any good parent, our God has His children's best interest in mind, nothing else. In an AIDS-infested society this realization ought to make more sense than in the free-love and free-sex society of the prior two decades. Now even talk-show hosts, star athletes, and some in the gay community are advocating abstinence, restraint, and "clean" (monogamous) sexual partners. In other words, they are trying to do exactly what God did in giving the Law—regulate our sexual behavior because of the inherent potential for destruction when wrongly used. What is being regulated in Leviticus 15:1-33, in particular, has to do with either normal nocturnal emissions or the emissions during masturbation or intercourse that fall on the bed sheets. The underlying assumption is that our sex-life has great importance to the living God.

God knows our hearts. He knows that without regulations we end up doing what others are doing, or just experimenting with whatever may give us momentary feelings of pleasure. Modern culture has reduced sexuality to the power of choice, however one wants to be oriented—whether gay, bi, or straight. The major prohibitions in Leviticus 18 and 20 with regard to the male phallus have to do with keeping creational distinctions. (On homosexuality, incest, bestiality, and adultery, see *The Masculine Journey* pages 58-65 for a full discussion—only a portion is excerpted here.)

I am opposed to any kind of gay-bashing, and I am deeply concerned that we will lose to AIDS such a large resource of human creativity, energy, and contribution that lies in our gay communities. That said, I must speak out of my own observation, research, counseling experience, and spiritual convictions. The penis has no place *in* another man.

God obviously knew men would be put into situations with men (close, isolated quarters) where this would be a very real temptation. The pleasure experienced in the playful moments of youth or the bonding that occurs through the first experience—subsequently repeated—does not change the reality of the creational order. The primary purpose of our sexuality is affirmed only through a relationship with the feminine counterpart in the institution of marriage. In rejecting the God-given opening of the woman, the gay man merely affirms what he thinks he is denying whenever he finds an alternate opening.

What about those gay men who say "God made me this way"? Certain men might have a greater predisposition toward homosexuality than other men. But predisposition is one thing, sexual orientation and practice are another. We heterosexuals have the predisposition to be adulterers every day! Many socializing forces interplay with whatever the biological factors are in this constellation of needs, wants, experiences, and choices.

Because men do not readily reveal their deepest sexual experiences, fears, or frustrations, they often have no idea about what is normative. We think "normative" is whatever our experience has been. In my counseling of gay men over the past twenty years, not one had a normative childhood or normative adolescent development in the sexual arena. Their masculinity was stolen, so they go looking for it in other men, trying to reunite their phallus with their own lost manhood.

However, just as Jesus made it clear that the real locus of adultery is in the human heart or mind (Matthew 5:28), so the phallus is stimulated by how the mind conceives the ultimate sexual experience. The role of fantasy in the phallic man is critical to understanding his fears, frustrations, and especially his sexual compulsions.

The Phallus and Male Fantasy

Warren Farrell, a controversial writer on men's issues, identifies man's primary fantasy as "having access to as many beautiful women as desired without risk of rejection." Women's primary fantasy, contrary to much of the popular women's literature, is that of "security and family." The sexual power that women have over men is often underestimated and rarely analyzed or talked about with other men. Yet men daily sacrifice careers, reputations, and marriages for the phallic pleasure that women can give. The pleasure is far more than sexual. It involves the affirmation, acceptance, and praise that the phallic male so desperately needs.

To be male is to be phallic. By creation we are either male *or* female. But to understand the full range of human sexuality is to understand that we are created male *and* female. This means learning to honor God with our phallus in the context of the restraints He has prescribed. This is for our own good. It means, as both married and single men, learning to sublimate and channel our sexual passion into things constructive and generative.

EXPLORING THE ISSUES WITH OTHER MEN

> **Note to the leader:** If the men in your group are likely to have difficulty talking vulnerably and empathetically with each other about their sex lives, then stop and talk about why you are having that difficulty.

1. Men grow up with confused models of sexuality. Yet the church has been strangely silent. (When was the last time you heard a sermon on the subject of the male phallus?) A potpourri of views from the media, peers, parents, public authorities, locker room buddies—even Leviticus and Robert Hicks—are listed here. Among these models, which ones from childhood and current sex education have you encountered? Which ones are you inclined to agree with? Which ones do you strongly disagree with?

   ◆ I am a male only if I *feel* like it.
   ◆ I am a male only if I *do* what my culture considers masculine.
   ◆ I am a male for the same reason the doctor exclaimed, "It's a boy!"
   ◆ Living as if all that matters is below your belt is abnormal and abhorrent.
   ◆ Anything goes, as long as you practice "clean" (monogamous) sex.
   ◆ Anything goes, as long as you practice "safe" (protected) sex.
   ◆ With my sex life I state who I am and what I worship and why.
   ◆ Our sex life matters to God, even what happens to our semen.
   ◆ I have no idea what "normative" male sexuality is like.
   ◆ Other:

2. Both heterosexuals and homosexuals fall back on the argument: "God made me this way." Using arguments from Scripture and *The Masculine Journey*, what would you say to a homosexual friend who really wanted to know what God created him to be?

3. Our culture has presented many initiation rites, or passages to manhood, that are associated with the phallus. Which ones have you experienced? Do you have a story to share with other men about one such event?

  ❑ When I was potty trained and stopped wetting my bed
  ❑ Pubic hair and growth
  ❑ An unfortunate experience with pornography
  ❑ My first dating experience
  ❑ My first really embarrassing moment with a girl
  ❑ The wedding night
  ❑ Conceiving my first child
  ❑ Other:

4. If only the church had alternative initiation rites to the ones offered above. What creative alternative celebrations can you think of?

5. The author develops his arguments in a way designed to provoke thinking and discussion. Subdivide into groups of three or four and pick one thought-provoking argument, restated below; then discuss its truth and application among yourselves.

❑ Getting stuck in Phallic City is not peculiar to puberty or oversexed dirty old men, but is a normal part of a developing manhood.

❑ The underground search for sexual fulfillment in topless nightclubs, endless affairs, gay bars, adult videos, and locker room bragging reflects a God-hunger deep within our psyche—a spiritual hunger that is universal, mysterious, and powerful.

❑ Various socializing forces, needs, wants, experiences, and choices interplay with whatever the biological factors are to predispose someone toward homo-sexuality or heterosexuality. This *predisposition* is different from sexual orientation or practice and should not be confused with *predetermination* ("God made me this way").

❑ Those men who end up gay did not begin that way, but they lack normative childhood or adolescent development in the sexual arena. Their homosexual flings are really an attempt to find their lost or stolen manhood. Promiscuous heterosexuals have the same problem.

❑ "Normative male sexuality" is best defined not in relative personal or cultural terms, nor by modern psychological or sociological measures, but only in absolute terms as stated in the Bible.

PROFILING A BIBLE CHARACTER

Samson, the judge of legendary strength, embodies the phallic man forever stuck at the sexual level of manhood, despite the fact that he was used mightily by the Lord to deliver Israel from the Philistines. Read Judges 13–16, then answer the questions that follow.

6. Despite his miraculous birth, his Nazirite vow of absti-nence and dedication (Judges 13:1-5; see Numbers 6:1-21), Samson failed to develop beyond the sexual level of man-hood. How come "many men get stuck in Phallic City" (as Hicks says)?

7. Even with the Spirit of the Lord upon him throughout his life (Judges 13:25; 14:6,19; 15:14), Samson lusted after and married a forbidden Philistine woman (14:1-4), and then avenged her betrayal with indiscriminate rage (14:19–15:8). How do you account for this strange power of the male phallus?

❏ The Spirit's empowering was intermittent, not permanent.
❏ Rules and regulations are powerless to control the urging in a man's loins.
❏ God had a redemptive purpose for leading Samson by his phallus.
❏ Samson rationalized his sexual choices as "God's will for his life."
❏ How would Samson know that sexual sin can be fatal?
❏ Love-hate relationships are common to all men, even believers.
❏ Samson experienced a "second adolescence" between marriages.
❏ Other:

8. a. Samson's passionate affair with the Philistine Delilah confirms our choice of Samson as the phallic man (Judges 16). Despite the power of the male phallus, Samson was powerless in relation to women. How do you account for this form of "impotence"?

b. If even spiritually empowered, physically endowed Samson had difficulty in this arena, what hope is there for the rest of us?

35

9. In what ways have the women in your life used the "if you really loved me" line? What crazy thing were you once willing to do in the name of love? (For example, did you ever sacrifice career, reputation, or marriage for the pleasures—acceptance and praise—of a woman?)

10. Man's primary fantasy is "having access to as many beautiful women as desired without risk of rejection," says Warren Farrell, who polled 106,000 men and women from all walks of life. Farrell also tabulated many secondary fantasies, some of which are listed here. From these options choose the one that best completes this sentence for you: "The daydream, wishful thinking, or primary fantasy that recurs for me is . . ."

❑ Access to beautiful women without risk of rejection.
❑ A partner who is a perfect "10" but is not stuck on herself.
❑ A partner who loves me unconditionally but pushes me to grow up.
❑ A job full of significance, challenge, and reward with time for family.
❑ A wife who brought home enough money so that I would not have to jump through all the hoops of a full-time job, but could be a full-time dad.
❑ Financial independence and the time to spend it all.
❑ Gaining the recognition that being a hero/top performer brings.
❑ Regaining the figure and romance I enjoyed on my wedding night.
❑ That everyone in church will rise up and call me blessed.

11. Warren Farrell's conclusion about the primary male fantasy may explain the power of pornography. It provides men with the ultimate fantasy fulfillment without the risk of emotional rejection that accompanies relations with "real" women. When have you experienced rejection by real women? What effect did this have on you?

❑ Sent me into a temporary tailspin.
❑ Sent me into a lifelong tailspin. I'm still a bachelor.
❑ Led me to "easy sex" in some other relationship.
❑ I licked my wounds and vowed sexual abstinence.
❑ I did pursue the primary male fantasy through
  pornography.
❑ I recovered my sexual sanity by healthier pursuits.
❑ Other:

This second stop on the male journey is not a temporary detour, for we never outgrow our phallus. Still we must move on and grow up. The next step looks at man's sexual and violent nature in terms of the warrior. The warrior is not just set on sexual or military conquests, but on getting that degree, succeeding in business, and making a name for himself. Read chapter 4 in *The Masculine Journey* for the next session. As we find and redefine ourselves in terms of the warrior, ponder these quotes:

> We are not interested in generals who win victories
> without bloodshed. . . . Sooner or later someone will
> come along with a sharp sword and hack off our arms.
> — Carl von Clausewitz, from *On War*

> What is a man without his sword?
> — Robert Bly, quoted in *To Be a Man*

In preparation for the next session, begin thinking about what worlds are set before you to conquer. Ask yourself what your life would be like "without your sword," with nothing to fight for.

TAKING IT FURTHER WITH OTHER STUDIES

◆ On the beauty of sexuality: Song of Solomon, Hosea
   3, Ephesians 5:21-33
◆ On the abuse of sexuality: Proverbs 5, 7; Hosea 1-2
◆ On control of sexuality: Matthew 19:1-12, 1 Corinthians 6:12-7:9
◆ Other Bible characters who embody themes of this
   session are Boaz (Ruth 1-4), David (2 Samuel 11-12),
   and Solomon (Song of Solomon). The latter two also
   portray other points of the masculine journey.

The Warrior—
Gibbor: The Glorious Hero

♦

IDENTIFYING THE ISSUES WITH ROBERT HICKS
Excerpted and adapted from *The Masculine Journey*, pages 71-94.

Men who never discover the warrior aspect of their being are not real men. They are what Robert Bly calls "mother-bound" boys still in need of a sword to cut their adult souls away from their mothers.

I am personally concerned when I see young men in their twenties already giving up the fight. Whether from dysfunctional family backgrounds, multiple job firings, or debilitating divorces, they are dead. The warrior-within has departed. They have lost their sword.

Popular Rejection of the Warrior
Battles, guns, bombs, swords, knives, blood—these accoutrements of the warrior are decried as violent by most women. The interesting irony is how women say they hate violence, yet love the conquering hero. Warriors are labeled as warmongers, baby-killers, and murderers. Much of the growing men's movement in the United States is about the recovery of the warrior, often to the dismay of feminists.

Gibbor: The Hebrew Warrior
Gibbor (Hebrew for "warrior") stands unapologetically throughout the Bible as one primary stop on the masculine journey. The root idea is that of power or strength with an emphasis on excellence and superiority. A warrior without strength is

38

a contradiction of terms. The psalmist confessed, "I am reckoned among those who go down to the pit; I have become like a man [*gibbor*] without strength" (Psalm 88:4). The language of the warrior influences how warriors perceive the world, engage people, and talk about any subject.

Gibbor is always used of grown men, never of women; in fact, to be likened to a woman is a serious putdown for a warrior (Jeremiah 30:6). Only men over thirty were called *gibborim* (1 Chronicles 23:3,24,27).

Competing to be superior, to be prominent, to gain significance—it's as if the sexual energy of the phallic stage has given birth to more vocational pursuits whereby the man wars in every area of his life. The warrior in men energizes them to keep going, to press toward goals, to stand their ground, to defend personal and corporate values, even to the point of risking self. As men we war in business, in sports, in marriage, in conversations, and with our political agendas.

The male warrior instinct cannot be dead because it is intrinsic, woven into the fabric of our being as men. I contend this is a normal and natural stop on the male journey, not to be despised or devalued by men or women. Men abused and defeated by life, take note that God is very much a warrior.

God as Warrior

Yahweh is characterized by warrior strength: "Great is Thy name in might [*gibbor*]" (Jeremiah 10:6); and "This time I will make them know My power and My might [*gibbor*]; and they will know that My name is the LORD [Yahweh]" (16:21). As a *gibbor*, God fights for righteousness, justice, faithfulness, and truth.

God is not passive, immobile, and unconcerned, never lifting His holy finger in violence. He fights for His people to liberate, save, protect, and sustain them. Often, from our modern perspective, God does things that seem unjust, even violent, but that is what the life of the warrior is all about, even for God.

The Messianic Warrior

God has given the power to governments to take life, whether in war or by capital punishment (Romans 13:1-4). Good government seeks to use this power in ways that are ethical and moral. But I do not believe that just war equals holy war. A holy war is when God tells us to fight in His name: as in the conquest of Canaan under the command of Joshua; and the final war of the world, where Christ Himself will wage war against God's enemies on earth (Revelation 19:11-19). The only wars that are truly holy are where God Himself has made the determination, and I believe in this present age we cannot know that.

Therefore, the only true warrior for God is the Messiah— *El-Gibbor*, or the mighty-warrior God. This waging of war by Christ is as redemptive as His dying on the cross. The warrior must be willing to shed blood, either his own or another's, in order to accomplish anything worthy of redemption. Redemption characterizes the national warriors and heroes who protect their societies.

Gibbor as National Warrior and Hero

Gibbor refers to the experienced veteran of combat or the hero status achieved by spectacular feats of bravery and making a name for oneself. *Gibbor*-strength is needed to win a race (Psalm 19:5), win a war (Isaiah 36:5), or gain material wealth and standing (2 Kings 15:20, Ruth 2:1).

The reign of David advanced the concept of the *gibbor* to that of a standing militia and a handpicked, elite corps of thirty warriors who protected the royal court (2 Samuel 10:9, 23:8-23). These were the most experienced, combat ready, and well-decorated special forces of their day. Solomon apparently continued the practice of having the royal elite guard, expanding it to sixty (Song of Songs 3:7-8).

Such is the pride of the few, the brave, the elite. When shared with comrades in arms, the bonding is powerful and virtually impossible to replicate in peacetime.

This camaraderie of brothers is severely missing today. Somehow the church has not been able to recreate Gideon's Three Hundred, David's Thirty, or the Twelve of Jesus Christ. God the Father and Christ are examples of what it is to be a warrior. We must embrace the latent or rejected warrior within ourselves, not only for our own development, but also for the sake of our society and the church. The warrior never serves himself. He is a servant of the king and his commander (1 Chronicles 29:24). Thus we must know what and who we serve. To be seen as a virtue, the physical power of the warrior must be in the service of a larger view of masculinity.

Gibbor as Spiritual Warrior

True manliness is being the spiritual warrior who does not trust in his own abilities or possessions but only in God (Psalm 34:8, 40:4; Jeremiah 17:5). God tells the defeated, suffering Job to gird up his loins as a warrior would do, preparing himself for battle (Job 38:3, 40:7). Like Job I need to respond to God as a warrior when He has a harsh word for me. The warrior lets God be God, and knowing his own position before the Lord, salutes smartly, and goes on to carry out God's task in the world.

The fight matures, the conflict ages, and the drawing of psychic blood develops the young phallic male into a *gibbor*, a warrior. For city boys, there are no more hunts, no more calling the boys from the villages of women, no more going out into the woods to kill one's first bear. So we must find our warrior courage in other ways to consider ourselves men.

Wherever the bears are in our lives, we must call forth the warrior within us to kill them. We trust God with the outcomes and risk psychological injury to self or others—all in order to become men. *What is a man without his sword?* In all the men's groups I have experienced, I am most encouraged by how they rally around another man to help him pick up the sword—whether in his work, his marriage, or dealing with his own demons from the past.

EXPLORING THE ISSUES WITH OTHER MEN

1. Think back through the important men in your life—your dad and granddads, teachers and coaches, golf and tennis partners, fishing buddies and fellow hunters, mentors and advisors. Picture the plaques, trophies, and awards that adorn the walls and desks of their respective rooms. Listen to their language, how they perceive the world and engage people. Choose one man and his warrior tokens to reflect on further and share with the group. As you picture him, what does he stand for or fight for?

2. a. Judging by the tokens of the warrior, what is it that you stand and fight for? Go ahead and brag a bit.

   b. Does your family, if any, credit you with those same hard-won victories? If not, what would they see as the "game of life" that you are trying to win?

3. Judging by the magazines men buy, the warrior aspect is not dead. The magazines listed below are best sellers among men. Which of these magazines have you browsed recently? What common themes do you see in this list?

   ❑ *VFW*
   ❑ *Money*
   ❑ *Playboy*
   ❑ *Golf Digest*
   ❑ *Outdoor Life*
   ❑ *American Legion*
   ❑ *American Hunter*
   ❑ *Field and Stream*
   ❑ *American Rifleman*
   ❑ *Sports Illustrated*

4. Perhaps you, or someone you know, do not have enough fight left in you to advance or defend yourself at work. Such men defeated by life do not even work for a better family, much less the cause of social justice. What about the growing men's movement could help such men?

   ❑ Warrior weekends (don't forget to bring your drums).
   ❑ A warrior's trophy case as a tribute to "my glory days."
   ❑ A performance review and kick in the pants by a warrior-manager.
   ❑ Bible studies that reveal the warrior nature of God and His people.

❑ Light a "fire in the belly" by recalling good warrior myths.
❑ Have my sword sharpened by a fellow warrior, as "iron sharpens iron."
❑ Issue a "call to arms" to join Christian warriors in. . . .

5. The ultimate spiritual reward for the *gibbor* is not in the honors, decorations, or medals he may obtain, but in the children God gives him (Psalm 127:4). The true warrior is pro-family. How is your warrior lifestyle evident in the things you do for and with your children?

❑ I live vicariously through my quiver full of children, as when they make the grades, the team, the college, or the money that I (never) did.
❑ I have a quiver full of kids, but I feel under attack all the time.
❑ I don't have any children, but I invest in other young people.
❑ I give my kids performance reviews and prod them to shape up.
❑ I bless my kids with the knowledge that I love them no matter what.
❑ Our family trophy case is a tribute to *their* glory days, not mine.
❑ Other:

PROFILING A BIBLE CHARACTER

David, the second king in Israel's history, epitomizes the warrior aspect of maleness. David's defeat of the Philistine warrior is legendary (1 Samuel 17). But what makes him the premier warrior in Scripture is all the lesser-known warrior acts buried in 1 Chronicles (11:4-25, 12:21-38, 18:1-13, 20:1-3, 21:1-17). Skim those Scriptures, then answer the following questions.

6. After slaying Goliath with his slingshot, David was celebrated throughout Israel. King Saul, who had killed only

"thousands," became angry and jealous of David's growing reputation for slaying "tens of thousands" (1 Samuel 18:6-9). When has competition with another warrior gotten the better of you and sent you into a bout with anger or jealousy?

❑ When I compared report cards with my fellow students.
❑ When I lost my girlfriend to another suitor.
❑ When a colleague was promoted over me.
❑ When a sister organization or church outperformed ours.
❑ When I saw the comparative sales or salaries of the other managers.
❑ Other:

After Saul died, King David marched on Jerusalem, where he established the new capital and issued a warrior-like challenge: "Whoever leads the attack on the Jebusites will become commander-in-chief" (1 Chronicles 11:6). Joab answered the call (by making the first kill, we assume) and thus was given charge of other *gibborim*. Strategist Joab began building David's ragtag militia into a forceful standing army (12:21-38). General Joab built a distinguished military career for himself in David's cabinet (19:8-15). Unfortunately, Joab became a ruthless blood avenger, killing Absalom against David's orders and plotting with Abonijah against David and Solomon. This man of violence had to die by violence (1 Kings 2:31).

7. a. When have you risen to the challenge offered by your boss and taken up "the sword" at work?

   b. What challenge to join the battle, or call to leadership, have you received from our Commander-in-Chief of spiritually armed forces?

c. When have you, like Joab, shed (psychological) blood without cause?

8. The violent-bloody realism of battle is found in the life of David, the *gibbor* who decapitated Goliath (1 Samuel 17:51), but also loved God, wrote poetry, played stringed instruments, danced, and wept. Does this image of a warrior surprise you? Men are taught not to show fear or tears. Do you?

9. David's greatest sin was not adultery with Bathsheba nor arranging the murder of Uriah (2 Samuel 11:2-5, 6-17). David's greatest sin was to muster all his warriors throughout Israel and have them counted (1 Chronicles 21:1-17). David's unwarranted census brought a plague on Israel that killed 70,000 innocent people, whereas the above two sins and their cover-up resulted "only" in two deaths—Uriah's and that of David's out-of-wedlock child.

   After David confessed his sin, God backed off the plague, yet the question remains: Why was numbering the military so evil in God's eyes?

   ❑ God is a God even of the trivial.
   ❑ The numbers were so large—1.3 million warriors at David's disposal (2 Samuel 24:9)—that David would rely on that and not need to trust God.
   ❑ It's prideful to know one's true warrior strength and capabilities.
   ❑ David had come a long way since the days of the single slingshot and needed to be brought low for his own good.
   ❑ David's greatest strength as a warrior was also his greatest vice.
   ❑ Warriors who shed blood will have nothing to do with building God's house (1 Chronicles 22:6-8).
   ❑ Other:

10. When has pride in your accomplishments and capabilities as a warrior gotten the better of you, as it did David? In God's eyes, what then might be your greatest sin? Confess that sin to God, especially if that sin may have blocked your ability to trust Him totally.

11. Men today must win certain battles to prove their manhood. This may involve "psychological blood," if not actual risk of injury or loss of life. When has this happened for you?

   ❑ When I first stood up to my abusive father (as when fourteen-year-old Bill Clinton told his stepdad to stop beating his mom).
   ❑ When I asked my mother to stop criticizing and made the decision to cut the apron strings.
   ❑ When I took control of my life and resisted manipulation by others.
   ❑ When I kicked my addictive habit and joined a recovery group.
   ❑ When I fought the law and beat the unfair justice system.
   ❑ When I bagged the company sales trophy.
   ❑ When I pummeled my body back into shape.
   ❑ When I beat the "big C" and went on living productive years.
   ❑ Other:

12. The pride of the warrior in warfare, athletics, and business brings out the best in a man. In what arenas were you most competitive as an emerging adolescent? As a young man? A middle-aged man?

   ❑ Crossing the finish line or scoring the winning point.
   ❑ Shooting my first bear (buck or whatever).

❑ Finally getting to kiss the girl of my dreams.
❑ Winning entrance to the school of my choice.
❑ Joining the battle with my comrades in arms.
❑ Closing a big deal.
❑ Doing the best for my family.
❑ Winning professional recognition for my career
   achievements.
❑ Other:

13. a. What spiritual victory, career, or family goal is the war-
    rior within you *still* striving to win? (Or have you given
    up on a major goal?)

   b. Unfortunately, some warriors do not know which bat-
    tles to fight and when to quit. What long-ago battles
    should you have quit by now (perhaps with an ex-wife
    or ex-boss)? If you can't think of any battles to quit
    fighting, ask for feedback from your group.

Usually it takes a tragic loss, or wounding experience, to move
a man out of the warrior perspective on his journey to manhood. Read chapter 5 in *The Masculine Journey*. As we look at
the wounded male in the next session, ponder these quotes:

   To be a man is to bear wounds and wear scars.
   —Patrick Arnold, in *Wildmen, Warriors, and Kings*

   I'm wounded but not slain, I will lay me down to bleed
   for a while.
   —John Dryden, from "Johnnie Armstrong's Last
   Goodnight"

In preparation for the next session, begin thinking through the
wounding experiences that have moved you from one place to
another on the masculine journey.

TAKING IT FURTHER WITH OTHER STUDIES

- On "just war" and "holy war": Deuteronomy 20, Joshua 6-11, Judges 3-16, Esther 8:1-9:17, Micah 4:1-5
- On fighting for social justice: Numbers 35, Proverbs 31:1-9, Isaiah 58, Ezekiel 22
- On spiritual warfare: Acts 4:23-31, Ephesians 6:12-20, Revelation 8:1-6
- On God's warrior nature: Psalm 18, 68, 106; Isaiah 25, 40, 59
- On Christ's warrior nature: Colossians 1:15-29; Revelation 1:9-19, 14:14-20, 19:11-21
- Other Bible characters who embody themes of this session are Joshua, Joab (2 Samuel 22-1 Kings 2), and Job.

The Wounded Male—
Enosh:
The Painful Incongruency

◆

IDENTIFYING THE ISSUES WITH ROBERT HICKS
Excerpted and adapted from *The Masculine Journey*, pages 97-120.

Wounding is a part of a man's life, but when wounded *real men don't cry*. Women suffer wounds the same as men, but they can cry, scream, and yell, and it's all considered normal. Men watch the painful barbs move through our lives without flinching. After all, the warrior is tough. But given enough wars, even the best of warriors end up being wounded.

Ancient Metaphors and Archetypes of Woundedness
Robert Bly roots the men's movement in the repressed pain we feel as the result of being wounded by life. To discover what manhood is all about, men must descend into the deep places of their own souls and find their accumulated grief.

Carl Jung uses the metaphor of the male of the species wounding himself through various forms of self-destructive behavior. For Jung, this is the only way that men come to grips with the reality that they are no longer the heroes they imagined in their youth. They must grow up as men by becoming "painfully aware" of their deep-seated wound.

Robert Fisher writes a somewhat humorous but convicting satire of a knight in rusty armor in search of his true self. He must rid himself of the rusty armor in which he is encased by encountering his own pain through a blow to the head.

In most primitive societies the males went through a formal puberty rite that required the experience of pain or wounding of

49

the body. Circumcision is a permanent wounding that reminds the boy that he is what he is—male. American Indians bonded by cutting fingers and mingling the blood to become "blood brothers." Fraternities have initiation ceremonies; the military has its boot camps.

From our first hours of maleness until we become adults, pain seems to be the doorway to manhood. Yet the wounded male experience, while common to most civilizations, is either denied or forgotten by Western culture. The emerging men's movement may be, at its roots, the attempt to reframe the wounding experience for men.

The Bible honors woundedness as a normal stop on the masculine journey. When a man encounters his wound, he wrestles with God.

Enosh: The Wounded Male

The Hebrew word *enosh* conveys the idea of being weak, feeble, and sometimes incurably sick, describing man's mortality, calamity, frailty, and fears (Isaiah 17:11, Jeremiah 17:16). The life of Job illustrates wounding in its most severe form—the loss of family, property, health, and wealth. The prayers of Moses and David also speak of this *enosh* kind of man, whose "days are like grass" (Psalm 103:15) and who will turn "back to dust." In the wounding experience I learn that I am not God, nor a little god, nor even a little bit like God. It is more the experience of wondering how or why God might have anything to do with me at all (Psalm 8:4).

Of course, women experience wounding in just as many ways as men, but this normative experience is more difficult for men to accept, talk about, and heal from. Why? On this point, both the biblical material and the contemporary literature support four conclusions.

Woundedness: The Deep Mortal Wound

Fundamentally, the wound is mortal, meaning a death experience. Every physical and psychic wound is one more small foretaste of death. Every time we feel pain, something dies within us. Men experience life with their bodies probably more than women, who experience life more emotionally and expressively.

The wound is profoundly spiritual. As such, the issues men are addressing are perhaps more theological in nature than those in the women's movement of the sixties.

The experience of midlife wounds may be the loss of jobs or loss of marriages, even the giving up of dreams and ambitions. Sam Keen believes all men are in some sense war-wounded. As such, we have developed well-crafted psychological armor that allows us to keep on functioning while not really healing. Many men are for the first time becoming more aware of the woundedness they have experienced in jobs, failed marriages, addictions, and their own families of origin.

Woundedness: Deep Loss Reactions

If we find significant male meaning in being the warrior and being phallic, then anything that defeats us in these two areas brings about a profound sense of loss. When wounded, we no longer quite know who we are.

Job was a warrior who had it all: wealth, a large family, a supportive wife, a large estate, friends, good health. Then one day, a cruel fate hit Job. Likewise, we can be hit by one cruel bullet, car accident, job phase-out, or spouse walking out. When wounded by life, we feel remorse for what has been lost, and we begin to live in a romantic past when things were better. This is exactly what Job did (Job 29:1–30:21).

Woundedness: Alienation and Incongruency

When a man is wounded by the blows of life, the wounding throws his sense of balance off. The wounded believer experiences a sense of distance and alienation even from God (Psalm 73:1-14). Extreme incongruency with God can lead to new understanding and respect for the mysterious ways of God (Psalm 73:15-28).

Animals, when hurt, try to remove themselves from the scene and isolate themselves, where they can privately lick their wounds and buy some time to heal. Perhaps we share some of this primal instinct. We men tend to isolate, buy time to nurse our woundedness, and don't want *anyone* to come near us. This reaction is often viewed as not wanting help or rejecting help, but I would say the reaction is distinctively characteristic of the wounded male.

Just as the wounded animal can begin to strike out at those who come near to give aid, so men can externalize their pain and manifest hostility, even violence, toward others.

Woundedness: Hostility and Violence

Whether wounded by society or circumstances, by parent or spouse, the hostile male feels powerless and so strikes out. The hostile spirit is rooted in woundedness. I am convinced many men in our society today are lashing out at women, at society, at bosses, even at God—all because they do not understand the wounding experience. Men must begin to see that out of woundedness comes significant healing, meaning, and growth.

Purple Hearts for Broken Spirits

In our enlightened American culture, we have devalued both the role of the warrior and his wounds. By awarding the purple heart, the military demonstrates something that civilians may still have trouble accepting. Being wounded needs to be recognized, praised, and awarded.

In the absence of cultural markers from fathers, wives, or institutions, we as men need to affirm and value the wounds ourselves. Perhaps only in the circle of the fellow wounded can purple hearts for broken spirits be awarded. *Enosh* City may become a stifling dead end or just a detour on the masculine journey. Or, from our time of wounding, we can emerge as rulers of our own souls.

EXPLORING THE ISSUES WITH OTHER MEN

1. For Robert Hicks the first memorable experience of wounding was as a five-year-old when his granddad took him fishing and the fishing hook pierced his finger. For you, what memorable flesh wounds signaled a passage to manhood?

   ❑ Submitting to circumcision (as an infant or an adult).
   ❑ Becoming a blood brother with a best friend.
   ❑ Bruises from stealing and sliding into "second base."
   ❑ Going under the knife to get my appendix, tonsils, or teeth taken out.
   ❑ Going through fraternity hazing.
   ❑ Getting tattooed.
   ❑ Surviving military boot camp.
   ❑ Other:

2. Many of us need a proverbial blow to the head with a two-by-four to jar us awake and bring us to our senses. Movies, television, and the press satirize men as bozos who "just don't get it" when it's obvious to everyone else (as when someone denies his alcohol or drug addiction until confronted by a crisis intervention team).

   If a media presentation were made of your life, what "I just don't get it" experience would the camera lens zoom in on? What "blow to the head" finally got through to you on that stubborn issue?

3. Job's struggle to make sense of his woundedness offers a rich commentary about the *enosh* experience we all go through. See especially Job 1–3, 6–7, 14.

   a. What losses do you share in common with Job?

   b. What sense have you been able to make of your most intolerable loss?

4. Since death is basic to human existence (Genesis 5, Psalm 90:3, Hebrews 9:27), why do we fight it, as if it would never take its toll on us? Why not seriously prepare for death instead of always pursuing the American Dream in warrior-like fashion?

   ❑ Preparing for death neither hastens nor delays its coming.
   ❑ There is no heaven, no hell, and no hurry.
   ❑ Heaven can wait, but the American Dream cannot.
   ❑ Bad things always happen to good people (like Job),

so why be good?
- ❏ Old soldiers never die, they just lose their reason for living.
- ❏ Other:

5. This chapter zeroes in on the question of why this normative wounding experience is so difficult for men to accept, talk about, and heal from. Consider these four reasons why this might be the case. Which of these is true to your experience? How so?

- ❏ Male woundedness is inexplicably deep, a type of mortal wound.
- ❏ Men's identity is so wrapped up in what we have and what we do, that we react to deep losses by questioning who we are.
- ❏ Wounded men experience a profound "creaturely" alienation from God, often mixed with a certain "incongruency of the soul."
- ❏ Wounded men, feeling powerless, will resort to hostility and violence.

PROFILING A BIBLE CHARACTER

The biblical patriarch Jacob epitomizes the wounded male. Jacob illustrates a young man having been severely wounded by a dysfunctional family system. For background information, skim Genesis 25:19-34, 27:1–33:20. The statements here are excerpted from *The Masculine Journey* (pages 117-119).

The first portion of this case study in dysfunctional family systems begins in the mother's womb (Genesis 25:19-26), carries on in the family kitchen (25:27-34), and hits a new low in the parents' bedroom (27:1-40). Sibling rivalry, parental favoritism, and fraudulent scams all conspire for Jacob to eventually receive the coveted patriarchal blessing reserved for the firstborn.

6. a. Why would Esau be considered a "real man's man," then and now?

b. What makes Jacob a typical "momma's boy"?

c. How does parental favoritism play into scandalous deception and nasty protectionism?

d. What is especially wounding about growing up without a father's blessing? About being deprived later in life of that valued blessing?

In the next installment of this case study (Genesis 27:41–33:20), we see Jacob on the run—fearful, guilty, alienated from friends, family and God—even though he supposedly had the valued blessing. Consider what this typical wounded male does all this time to affirm that he is legitimately blessed before men and God:

◆ Jacob represses the hurt from his family of origin by staying away.
◆ He sells himself short to Laban, who out-schemes the schemer.
◆ He reproduces dysfunctional family roots in succeeding generations.
◆ He practices self-deception, as well as continuing to deceive others.
◆ He dreads a reunion with the sibling he once abused, and appeases him.
◆ He is so insecure in his standing with God and his brother he must prove he can still wrestle and win over whoever comes across his path.

◆ A blessing stolen through deception and parental favoritism does not count for much, but a blessing secured by God comes with a wounded hip.

7. Which of the above strategies relate closely to your experience?

Many men wrestle strangers in the night vainly searching for the blessing withheld. Jacob's elusive blessing and wounded hip are important metaphors on the masculine journey, reminding us that the wounding experience need not be negative, but can be a time of wrestling with God to see what life is all about.

8. a. How have you suffered from a blessing withheld?

b. When has God used a wounding in your life to bless you?

BRINGING IT HOME TO YOURSELF AND OTHER MEN

9. a. Why does it take so long to heal the masculine soul? Many answers have been proposed. Which of these have merit for men you know?

❑ Women put their men up on pedestals (strong successful heroes), yet pull us down with manipulative guilt and reminders of clay feet.
❑ Our fathers stoically stuffed all their hurt feelings and never modeled how they healed from their wounds.
❑ As men we have well-crafted psychological armor that allows us to function but inhibits healing.
❑ We are instinctively like animals, who isolate themselves and buy time to lick their wounds.
❑ The devil stalks our souls.

❏ God wants to, but can't do anything about my problem of pain.
❏ God could, but chooses not to do anything about my pain.

b. How would you counsel men who claim to suffer for these reasons?

c. Which of these rationales describes your own wounding experience?

The problem of male hostility and violence is rooted not in men's power over women, but in men's sense of powerlessness, stemming from deep woundedness. This explains why some men feel they must resort to abusing and using women, but does not condone this striking-back behavior.

10. a. Given this explanation, how then would you propose to treat or cure violent male offenders?

b. Have you taken this cure yourself?

11. For men to survive their wounding, they need to feel safety among fellow sufferers. How can you improve the dynamics in groups of men so that men would feel that safety and start sharing their pain?

❏ Have the pastor model his own woundedness from the pulpit.
❏ Have other men in power ("bully pulpits") share their heart wounds.
❏ Create a Christian fellowship of soldiers, athletes, or businessmen whose ticket for admission is the admission of wounds (as in "AA").

❑ Sponsor more AA-type recovery groups for the man in the pew.
❑ Create "Purple Heart Awards" for broken spirits, not just war wounds.
❑ Other:

When we're done licking our wounds and ready for more wholeness, we are ready for the next destination on the male journey. From our time of wounding we can emerge as rulers of our own souls. Read chapter 6 in *The Masculine Journey*. As we look at the mature male, ponder these quotes:

No one gets to adulthood without a wound.
—Robert Bly, from *Iron John*

I never thought I'd lose, I only thought I'd win.
—Elton John, from "The Last Song"

In preparation for the next session, begin thinking through the greater sense of direction and purpose in life that comes only with maturity and adversity.

TAKING IT FURTHER WITH OTHER STUDIES

◆ On the origin of suffering and evil: Job 1–2, 5:17-27, 33:12-30; Isaiah 14:3-23; Matthew 4:1-11
◆ On redemptive suffering: Leviticus 16:1-34, 1 Kings 8:33-53, Isaiah 52:13–53:12, Hosea 2:1-23, Mark 2:1-12, Romans 8:12-18, Hebrews 2:9-18
◆ On human frailty and mortality: Genesis 5; 2 Kings 20:1-11; Job 14:10-22; Psalm 49:10-19, 90; Ecclesiastes 2:1-16; 2 Corinthians 4:8-18; 1 Peter 2:18-25
◆ Other Bible characters who embody themes of this session are Saul (deserved suffering; 1 Samuel 13–15, 18–19, 22–24, 28, 31), Job (undeserved suffering), Jeremiah (Jeremiah and Lamentations), and Hosea.

The Mature Man—
Ish: The Reborn Ruler

◆

IDENTIFYING THE ISSUES WITH ROBERT HICKS
Excerpted and adapted from *The Masculine Journey*, pages 121-142.

We are not really prepared to be defeated by life. Therefore, when we are unexpectedly defeated we cave in and feel very out of control, slaves to our wounds. The good news is: The spirit can be reborn; the pains experienced in woundedness can be birth pangs anticipating the next destination on the male journey. Maturity springs only from adversity (James 1:12). It leads to the mature man, the resurrected ruler of the soul, the *'ish* kind of man.

The Meaning of *Ish*
The fifth Hebrew word in our study, *'ish*, is usually translated "man," "mankind," or "husband." Holladay's lexicon lists additional meanings: "those of higher rank, a ruler of lower rank, and man of God." *'Ish* stands in contrast with *yeled* (young man), *na'ar* (youth), and *zaken* (old man or sage), thus conveying the idea of the adult male or mature man.

Ish as the Attribual Male: One Known by His Attributes
'Ish describes a man by some attribute. He is a man of bravery (1 Samuel 4:9, 26:15), a man of good presence, "good looking" (1 Samuel 16:18), a man of kindness (Proverbs 11:17), a man of either smooth skin or hairy skin (Genesis 27:11). He may be known by his understanding (Proverbs 17:27), peacefulness (Psalm 37:37), or trustworthiness (Exodus 18:21). In ref-

erence to a man's occupation, calling, or social position, he is listed as a man of the priesthood (Leviticus 21:9), a man of the king or prince (Exodus 2:14), or a man of war (Deuteronomy 2:14). *'Ish* is used more often than any other term for the title "man of God" (seventy-five times). These references suggest that the mature man is the man known by his attributes, who has stopped trying to be the man others want him to be.

Integration

Psychologist John Friel asked men what they really wanted in themselves as men. (For a summary of his findings as published in *The Grown-up Man*, see question 2, page 63.) The findings reveal a deep-seated desire in men to be more integrated within themselves. They want a wider range of possibilities than they are presently experiencing. Each man wants a greater unity in his life.

Differentiation

The word *'ish* is also used with reference to the husband of a woman. This brings out the issue of differentiation. My personal view of a boy's developmental journey toward manhood rests primarily on the issue of differentiation. For a boy to become a man he must first break free from his mother and find his father. A woman can never make a boy into a man, whether it be the first mother or the second substitute mother, his wife.

For some men, differentiation may not be related to the family of origin or their current family relationships. It may relate to those times when I am being pushed into someone else's agenda or dream for my life, having to be someone I am not. Daniel Levinson calls this differentiation of maleness "detribalization." We are all tribalized by parents, teachers, pastors, churches, systems of thought, and friends.

Individualization

Maturity requires not only differentiation, or knowing what one is not, but also individualization, learning what one *is*. This is an essential requirement for men to survive the midlife transition period. The warrior doesn't factor in failure or weigh the ethics of warfare, he just fights. But men who have grown through their woundedness, and learned the critical issues that only woundedness can teach, have a more mature vision and dedication.

Dedication

The saddest men I know are the men who have no real vision for their lives. The man who goes to work every day, comes home, reads the paper, has dinner, watches television, and goes to bed—only to repeat the pattern the next day—is not alive or well.

We are Prince Charles looking for our Diana. But then we get wounded, bored, and frustrated. Disturbing questions, lingering from my wounding period, try to convince me to quit, change careers, and go get a real job.

It is the mature, *'ish*-kind of man who begins to rekindle the dream, modify the original vision, and return to the dedication lost in *Enosh* City (Woundedville). The *gibbor* is full of intense dreams—to win, to be right, to achieve, to be highly regarded—but with wounding these begin to fade. Yet with reflection, integration, differentiation, and individualization, a man can begin to dream again. By reappraising our attributes, we are in a better position to continue our growth more wholistically. The mature man finds a new symmetry to life, a new depth and richness not experienced before. He is a newly emerging relational man.

Ish as Relational Man

One of my criticisms of the current state of counseling is that the proposed cure for codependent relationships is that the client must so individualize and differentiate from the dependent relationship that very little responsibility to the spouse is left intact. The entire focus is centered on "breaking free." People in biblical relationships always have some feeling of being responsible for another human being and wanting to maintain connection with that person. This is precisely what is seen in other uses of *'ish*.

'Ish is commonly used with a similar sounding word, the word for woman, *'ishah*. Adam names his wife by adding a feminine ending to his own name *'ish* (Genesis 2:23). This may imply that she is like him (human). She is not an animal to be lorded over.

With the mature man, this idea of equality has a greater potential for realization. In contrast, the warrior builds relationships around power, authority, or "chain of command." Phallic man can easily join with *'ishah* in sexual intercourse, but there is seldom any real joining of spirits, and this makes her more an object than a person of equal stature. The wounded male usually becomes impotent in his significant relationships. He isolates himself to lick his wounds and, like an animal, growls when anyone comes near.

From this perspective, we may conclude that only the mature man can experience a sexual relationship with his wife that is based on complete, unabashed union of spirits. When both partners are no longer playing games, they know themselves and each other very well, and a new sexual freedom sets in. I have heard from older mentors that the best sex is yet to come. I can't wait!

'Ish is seen not only in marital relations but also in a man's national and communal relations (Exodus 21–22, Numbers 25:6, Judges 10:1, Proverbs 18:24). The mature man is involved in civic responsibilities, with friends, his culture, his tribe, and his nation. By these things he is known and valued. He is becoming a royal kind of person, taking back some rulership of life.

Ish as Royal Man

Individuals of rank or royalty, priests, prophets, and messengers from God are often called *'ish elohim,* or man of God. Although *'ish elohim* occurs seventy-five times in the Old Testament, describing such diverse men as Moses (Deuteronomy 33:1), Samuel (1 Samuel 9:6), Elijah (1 Kings 17:18), Elisha (2 Kings 4:7-13), and David (Nehemiah 12:24), ironically there is no uniform criteria by which the term "man of God" was applied to these men.

This raises the issue of whether a young man can really be a "man of God" in the sense of the royal man. Royal requirements take time to develop. David's life shows that a mature king, as well a mature man, is one who rules his life with the wisdom of Scripture. He is required to meditate on God's Word daily—tuning out other voices (Psalm 1).

EXPLORING THE ISSUES WITH OTHER MEN

1. We expect to win—whether it be in football, our marriages, our businesses, or getting out of an icy driveway. You are not a real man if you expect to lose. What unexpected losses, or defeats in life, have spurred you toward maturity?

❑ I was suddenly laid off or fired from work.
❑ I suffered a reversal of fortune (stocks, health, dating scene, etc.).
❑ I was seriously harmed by others (libel, lawsuit, injury, etc.).
❑ My attempts to win (promotion, prize, reelection, etc.) were defeated.
❑ I lost my family dream (miscarriage, divorce, teen suicide, etc.).
❑ Other:

2. Robert Hicks consulted one psychologist who cited findings that reveal a deep-seated desire in men to be more integrated within themselves. To gauge which of these findings reflects a deep-seated desire within you, rate your feelings about the following statements on a scale from 1 (who me?) to 5 (that's my hot button):

a. I want to feel more.   1 2 3 4 5

b. I want to befriend more.   1 2 3 4 5

c. I want to learn to love.   1 2 3 4 5

d. I want to find meaningful work.   1 2 3 4 5

e. I want to father significantly.   1 2 3 4 5

f. I want to be whole.   1 2 3 4 5

g. I want to heal and reconcile.   1 2 3 4 5

3. Robert Hicks contends that a boy's developmental journey toward manhood rests completely on the issue of differentiation. This journey involves several tasks. Which tasks have you already done? Which are you still working on?

❑ Not yet free of Mom, I am having trouble finding a wife.
❑ I found a wife who has become like a second mother to me.

❑ I have finally broken free from Mom and other mother figures.

❑ I am helping my son (or someone else's) break free of his mom.

❑ I am responsible for my family and want to stay connected.

❑ I am still conforming to someone else's agenda or dream for my life.

❑ I am not doing "my own thing," rather the opposite of someone I despise.

❑ I am my own person, no longer emulating or despising someone else.

4. An essential requirement for men to survive the mid-life transition period is to learn who we are, not just who we are not. That requires a certain individualization. Only God knows us perfectly, even our self-knowledge is distorted. Yet we can profit from this exercise. In the space below, write ten *nouns* that describe the roles you perform. Then write ten *attributes* that describe you, perhaps words that you have heard applied to you by others. Then turn to the person next you and begin characterizing yourself with no rebuttal.

Ten *Nouns* That Say
Who I Am
e.g., little league coach

Ten *Attributes* That Say
How I Am
e.g., enthusiastic

5. a. Do you know what it is that drives you, that makes you want to get up in the morning, that enables you to hang in there during this span of years called life? Write it down in one sentence.

   b. Is this vision clear to your loved ones?

PROFILING A BIBLE CHARACTER

Elijah, the prophet of God who defeated the prophets of Baal, embodies the wounded warrior who grows up and mentors another younger man. He portrays the qualities and comes through the stages that typify the mature man. Read 1 Kings 17–19 and 2 Kings 1–2. The statements below about Elijah are excerpted from *The Masculine Journey* (pages 143-147).

The young Elijah does everything God tells him to do and presto, God comes through miraculously in the supernatural multiplication of food and raising of the widow's son from the dead (1 Kings 17). Not a bad start for a young warrior-prophet! With success in small ministries, Elijah is now ready for the big time. God calls him to take on the Canaanites—King Ahab and the prophets of Baal.

6. All the classic elements of the warrior's challenge—emotion, drama, victory, pomp, and courage—are evident in 1 Kings 18. What examples of each can you find in that chapter?

7. Meanwhile, back at the office (19:1-2), when Ahab tells his wife, Jezebel, what happened, she goes ballistic and initiates a Mafia hit on Elijah. Elijah runs for his life. Why should this brave, victorious warrior be afraid now?

❏ Jezebel was more powerful than the women in Sidon, King Ahab, and the 450 prophets of Baal combined.
❏ Elijah lapsed in faith and forgot how miraculously God had delivered him in the past.
❏ Men naturally avoid conflict with irate, verbally threatening women.
❏ We all run out of gas finally; better to run out when going down hill.
❏ Nothing unusual here; spiritual lows always follow spiritual highs.
❏ Evidently, Elijah concluded, God would not come through this time.
❏ Other:

8. a. All the classic elements of wounded male behavior—retreat, licking wounds, self-pity, depression, giving up the cause—are evident in 1 Kings 19:3-10. What examples of each can you find?

    b. When have you felt or acted likewise?

9. God responds to this wounded warrior in ways that show Father knows best (19:15-18). Which of the following initiatives from God to Elijah have you experienced in your life?

    ❏ God rehabilitates a man by meeting physical needs for rest and food.
    ❏ God rallies a man with a focusing question about what drives him.
    ❏ God represents Himself in quiet, obvious ways, not in special effects.

☐ God rejects a man's resignation speech and poor-me pity party.
☐ God renews the vision to carry on a mature man's ministry.
☐ God recommissions a man to mentor the next generation.
☐ God reassures a man with a network of equally devoted colleagues.

BRINGING IT HOME TO YOURSELF AND OTHER MEN

Robert Hicks is typical of many men in mid-life when he identified the disturbing questions that break into his consciousness: Why are you teaching this? Do you really believe this? Who are you to be saying that? You don't really have anything to give, do you? Such questions will linger from our wounding period, trying to convince us to quit or change careers.

10. Consider God's focusing question to Elijah: "What are you doing here?" (19:9,13). Answer this question for yourself, as it applies to your current stage of life.

11. Robert Hicks contends that *'ish* becomes *'ish elohim* much later than is usually taught in other models of the male journey or the Christian life. For the royal declaration "man of God" to be true of any man, in fact, takes a record of deeds done, life blows, and wilderness periods. By this criteria, how might you qualify as a "man of God"?

A real man, such as Elijah, grows up in his relation to others and becomes the ruler of his own once-depressed soul. Because he has been wounded and recovered through hearing the Word of God in a refreshingly different way, Elijah is reborn and resurrected in his spirit. The mature man is then ready to be mentor and sage to a younger man. Read chapter 7 in *The Masculine Journey*. As we look at the fulfilled man, ponder these quotes:

Delighted to be but wise,
For men improve with the years.
—William Butler Yeats, "Men Improve with the Years"

Give me a young man in whom there is something of
the old, and an old man with something of the young;
guided so, a man may grow old in body, but never
in mind.
—Cicero, from *De Senectute*, XI

In preparation for the next session, begin thinking through your
roles at home, at work, at church, or in the community. In which
area could you be a mentor and take greater responsibility for
the next generation?

TAKING IT FURTHER WITH OTHER STUDIES

- ◆ Why did God call each of these a "man of God"?
  Moses (Deuteronomy 33:1), Samuel (1 Samuel 9:6),
  Elijah (1 Kings 17:18), Elisha (2 Kings 4:7-13), and
  David (Nehemiah 12:24) *Hint:* The reasons vary with
  each man.
- ◆ Other Bible characters who embody themes of this
  session are Joseph (Genesis 37-50), Isaiah (with a
  focus on Isaiah's call and the servant songs), and
  Daniel.

The Sage—
Zaken: The Fulfilled Man

◆

IDENTIFYING THE ISSUES WITH ROBERT HICKS
Excerpted and adapted from *The Masculine Journey*, pages 149-166.

As I compare three images of elders, I prefer the Middle Eastern motif. The biblical sage, or *zaken*, has far more in common with Middle Eastern Bedouin elders than with anything we currently see in American church life or retirement communities.

Zaken: A Word Study of the Gray-Headed Man
Zaken, the sixth Hebrew word for man in our study, has as its primary meaning "beard," but also carries the idea of being old or becoming old. Its meaning is associated with being gray and with legal competence in the community. The *zaken* also represented various social groups: cities (Deuteronomy 19:12), regions (Judges 11:5-11), tribes (1 Samuel 30:26), or nations (Numbers 11). This representative elder has nothing to do with our modern concept of the retired, uninvolved senior citizen.

Zaken as the Goal of Manhood
One modern tragedy affecting men is that they are burning out at such alarming rates. The Scriptures provide us with a much longer look at this thing called manhood: At forty, we are just kids!

After his third forty-year career stint, Moses wrote a song to teach the nation of Israel to remember what God had done for them: "Remember the days of old; consider the years of all generations. Ask your father, and he will inform you, your elders [*zakenim*], and they will tell you" (Deuteronomy 32:7). In other words, when one generation is on the verge of denying the ability of God to do something, bring in the elders! They have the knowledge, history, and experience with God to know what really happened, how God works, and how you should trust Him today. This has more to do with what we have learned from life than what we have accomplished.

The goal is to be a gray-headed old man who has some wisdom to pass on to the next generation. Of course, just because one has obtained a certain age or a head of silver hair does not mean they are wise (Psalm 119:100, Job 32:6-9). Study of the Scriptures, faith in God, trust in Christ, and obedience to biblical truth—without these, the elderly life can be empty, dry, uninteresting.

Even though we no longer live in a culture that honors the gray head or the senior citizen (besides giving them some discounts), it is encouraging to note the biblical perspective on aging:

> "Honor your father and your mother, that your days may be prolonged in the land which the LORD your God gives you." (Exodus 20:12)

> "Rise in the presence of the aged, show respect for the elderly and revere your God. I am the LORD." (Leviticus 19:32, NIV)

> Listen to your father, who begot you, and do not despise your mother when she is old. (Proverbs 23:22)

If obeyed, this one category of biblical admonition could radically change our culture and the treatment of parents, grandparents, and seniors in the United States.

To be a man of wisdom late in life is an honorable station, one that should be respected by the younger men, even though they may not respond to it positively.

Zaken as the Time of Genuine Fulfillment
I am convinced most Americans look for fulfillment in all the wrong places and at all the wrong times. When it comes to unfulfilled expectations, I see Christians just as frustrated

as anyone else. Whether one has mortgage payments, business loans, kids in college, or other responsibilities to meet, I wonder if anyone has any sense of fulfillment. Perhaps the time of genuine fulfillment is far ahead of where we think it should be.

Most of us don't think about how we want to die. We live in a death-denying culture. From the biblical perspective, the *zaken* stage is the time for ultimate fulfillment. Real fulfillment lies in going to a natural death with our business taken care of and our important relationships reconciled. This is, of course, the ideal. For the most part, dying people are cantankerous, bitter, demanding, and loaded down with regrets about almost everything. Certainly, the bitter spirits and regret can't be blamed totally on the physical ailments and diseases they are facing.

The Scriptures list three conditions that make the *zaken* time of life less than fulfilling. The first has to do with having no *zakens* in the family line. A messenger from God informed Eli that no man in his family would ever see the *zaken* stage of life (1 Samuel 2:30-34). Our later years are more fulfilling when we have family members around to age with. A second cause for the lack of fulfillment is grieving the needless loss of life due to unnatural causes. On his deathbed David alluded to the unnatural deaths that Joab had engineered (1 Kings 2:5-6). The third detriment to fulfillment is suffering the loss of our own young children. The pain of losing yet another son was too great for Jacob (Genesis 42:38). The gray-headed man does not want to go to his grave knowing that his own sons have preceded him in death.

What these obstacles to fulfillment have in common is the loss of life and of family connection. These become much more critical issues as one gets older. This gets at our own ability to suffer loss and move on from it. We certainly can't prevent the loss of family members as we get older, but we can perhaps do some preparatory inventory work about what loss represents to us.

Reconciliation

The key to experiencing *zaken* as the most fulfilling time of life is in having our important relationships maintained and reconciled. As promiscuous phallic men, insensitive warriors, and isolated wounded males, we men can make a mess of our primary relationships during our young- and middle-adult years.

To make our last years of life satisfying, we should do our best to reconcile any relationships severed or harmed in our earlier years.

Zaken as Time of Significant Contribution

We men are often very shortsighted and in a hurry. If we think life is over at forty, fifty, sixty, seventy, or even at eighty, we're wrong! The *zaken* of Israel were called together to defend their region (Judges 11:5-11), families, and cities (2 Kings 10:1-5). *Zaken* furnished counsel along with the priests and prophets (Ezekiel 7:26, Job 12:20, Jeremiah 18:18). Their decisions governed issues such as capital punishment and marriages (Deuteronomy 21:1-9, 25:5-10). The *zaken* also had some official capacity to oversee the faithful administration of the law (31:9,28).

This time of life is characterized by significant contribution, and probably the greatest contribution lies in the mentoring experience.

Mentoring

In almost every field today the concept of mentoring is being discussed. In the past it seemed everyone was content to pursue career goals individually without considering the role of others who might enhance the process. We have found that the mentor contributes several things to his students: a brain to pick, a shoulder to cry on, and an occasional kick in the pants. Beyond this, the mentor cares for the younger man in the *totality* of his life, and wants to see him become successful in life. I believe this is the greatest need in the church today.

EXPLORING THE ISSUES WITH OTHER MEN

1. Robert Hicks presents the model of the Middle Eastern sage for us to emulate. What do you think of that model—for yourself and your church—in comparison with the other two, as illustrated in the lists that follow?

Middle East Bedouin Tent Fellowship Model

◆ May appear to be shooting the breeze, but the random relational approach is a mix of social hospitality, business wheeling and dealing, personal counsel, and administrative justice.

72

- The young come to learn from the older men about business, marriage, sex, politics, and how to get the most mileage out of a camel.
- Wise men are old, but not retired or isolated.
- Wise men are involved in nurturing, leading, modeling, contributing.

American Suburban Church Model of Elders
- Runs on the business model, complete with agenda, minutes, and Robert's Rules of Order.
- Very little true hospitality, only coffee.
- No pillows, but a table made more for business board meetings.
- Most of the men do not have beards, nor gray hair. Most are white-collar executives still in the warrior stage of manhood.
- With a few exceptions, the meetings could be for General Motors, except we open with prayer and have a devotional.

The Retirement Community Model
- The gray-headed, bearded old man is well past his prime.
- Our culture sees senior citizens not as wise, but as barely competent.
- To be a wise, old man someday is not the chief aspiration of young men, but is disdained or avoided.
- Seniors are huddled in enclaves separated from the mainstream of society and the young.
- They play golf, bridge, watch reruns, and wait for their kids to call.

2. a. Of all the places on the masculine journey, which for you is the goal of manhood, place of genuine fulfillment, and time of most significant contribution?

   b. Do you know anyone who lives up to the ideal for the *zaken* stage of life? Describe that person to the group.

3. Suppose you were to adopt the long view of this thing called manhood. You might then conclude with Robert Hicks: At forty, we're just kids! At the age we call midlife, Moses was just beginning his second of three forty-year career stints: shepherding Jethro's sheep in Midian (yet to come was his third forty-year career stint shepherding God's people).

   a. What were (are) you hoping to accomplish by the time you hit forty?

   b. What would you like to do with the last two-thirds of your life?

   c. What are you going to do about unfulfilled expectations as you fall short of pulling off the American Dream?

4. The biblical perspective on aging is derived from several texts. What do these verses tell you about the *zaken* stage in life?

   Genesis 15:15

   Genesis 25:8

Exodus 20:12

Leviticus 19:32

1 Samuel 2:30-34

Psalm 92:12-15

Proverbs 16:31

Proverbs 17:6

Proverbs 23:22

5. Robert Hicks challenges us on the biblical view of aging: "If obeyed, this one category of biblical admonition could radically change our culture and the treatment of parents, grandparents, and seniors in the United States." Apart from ensuring a greater longevity for ourselves, what changes do you think would happen if Americans equated older age with prime of life?

6. Other than sound biblical teaching, what would have to happen for this country to shift its whole perspective on aging from viewing prime time as age forty to seeing life as beginning at age seventy or eighty? (What changes would have to take place in consumer ads? In media coverage? In the church boards? In attitudes toward gray hair?)

PROFILING A BIBLE CHARACTER

The "mentor-student" relationship is so badly needed in the church today. Our first biblical profile is the relationship between Elijah and Elisha. Review 1 Kings 19:1-21 and read 2 Kings 1:1-2:18, before answering the questions that follow. (Hicks develops a second biblical profile of the *zaken* man in the career of Abraham, who had elder responsibility for the welfare and continuance of his family. Read *The Masculine Journey* pages 167-171 for further application and insight of this model.)

7. Note how Elijah's character and experience qualify him as a classic mentor.

◆ Maturity and renewed vision is born out of a wounding experience.
◆ Obeying God in small and large steps of faith.
◆ Despite his efforts to turn in his prophet's badge, the mantle of leadership is still on Elijah.
◆ Just as Elijah thought he was through, God focuses his attention on a younger prophet, whom he is to anoint.

a. Which of these aspects of being a mentor have you personally benefited from in someone else?

b. Which of these qualities make you a potential mentor to someone?

8. On the other end of the Elijah-Elisha relationship, note what makes Elisha a classic student, capable of learning from a mentor.

◆ Mentoring was pursued by Elisha, who was always at Elijah's side.

76

- ◆ Elisha recognized and requested a double portion of Elijah's spirit.
- ◆ Elisha hangs around long enough to get what he wants.
- ◆ Discipleship is better "caught" than "taught," and Elisha caught it.

   a. Which of these aspects of being a student have you personally put into practice?

   b. Which of these qualities make you a good student for some mentor to take under his wing?

Several painful, character-developing, faith-testing experiences matured Abraham as a mentor for his family: (1) giving up the object of his dreams (Genesis 22); (2) losing a spouse and becoming a single parent (Genesis 23); (3) finding a proper spouse for his child (24:1-9,62-67); (4) wanting a legacy for his children (25:1-8).

9. What character-developing, faith-testing experiences, as illustrated by Elijah or Abraham, have you seen in a true-to-life *zaken* that you know?

BRINGING IT HOME TO YOURSELF AND OTHER MEN

10. What plans have you made for your death? Use this checklist to assess your state of readiness.

77

❑ My business dealings are taken care of, thanks to financial planning.

❑ My important relationships are reconciled.

❑ I have made provision to care for any dependents who survive me.

❑ Through my wounding I now know how to suffer loss and move on from it.

❑ I am my own nurturer and have broadened my base of relationships so that the loss of family will not devastate me.

❑ I have made provision for my soul, thanks to Christ.

❑ I have bought a burial plot and made other funeral arrangements.

❑ I have composed what I want put on my tombstone.

❑ I have extended the blessing to the next generation by telling them face to face, and through my prayers, that they will succeed.

❑ I have included that blessing in my last will and testament.

❑ I vow not to be cantankerous, bitter, demanding, or regretful in old age.

11. Robert Hicks contends that the greatest need in the church today is for mentors. In your stage in life, are you looking for others who might help you pursue your life goals? Or are you looking for a "student" to help in the process?

    Place a name next to the need that you want to see fulfilled in your life by some mentor. If you think of someone you could help in regard to a specific need, put his name down as well.

    ◆ The mentor whose brain you would like to pick.
    ◆ The mentor whose shoulder you could cry on.
    ◆ The mentor whose occasional kick in the pants would be welcome.
    ◆ The mentor who cares for the totality of your life and wants you to become successful in life.

We have just concluded the last stop on the masculine journey. You are now ready to die! All that remains for you is to make a commitment to join Christ on this new male journey. Read chapter 8 in *The Masculine Journey*. As we look at the ultimate male model, Jesus Christ, ponder this final quote:

> And ah for a man to arise in me
> That the man I am may cease to be!
> — Lord Alfred Tennyson, from *Maud*

In preparation for the final session, begin thinking about how Jesus embodies the various character traits of the different men along the journey.

TAKING IT FURTHER WITH OTHER STUDIES

- ◆ On aging, gray hair, mentoring, preparing for death, leaving a legacy, and so on, check a concordance for possible Bible references.
- ◆ As a foreshadow to our discussion in session 8, you may want to study these relationships: Jesus with Peter, Barnabas with Paul, Paul with Timothy.

A New Male Journey

◆

IDENTIFYING THE ISSUES WITH ROBERT HICKS
Excerpted and adapted from *The Masculine Journey*, pages 173-183.

Dorothy-types like to stay on the yellow-brick road, keep moving, and can't wait to get where they are going. Winnie-the-Pooh-types just enjoy the trip, the people they meet along the way, and the experiences. They feel a little regret when the trip is over. You may have felt like one or the other as you've followed the male journey. The six stages along the way are unique for each man, but they have some important commonalties. Just as each stage has some crucial new issues a man must face, so also each stage demands new applications of faith in response to the *ultimate masculine model*.

Confusion
The *'adam* kind of man may be confused by having to unravel and integrate the paradoxes of human potentiality and sinful tendencies. We may struggle with our own mortality and unfulfilled yearnings.

For the phallic man, the *zakar*, confusion may exist in the emerging adolescent's sexuality, especially understanding what is normal for the adult male, whether married or not.

The *gibbor*, the warrior, may suffer confusion in trying to bring strength and intimacy together. The *enosh*, the wounded male, wonders how can he feel so vulnerable to pain and also be masculine.

The *'ish*, the mature man, experiences confusion about

80

what to do with the rest of his life, knowing he no longer has the same energy or tolerance. For the *zaken*, the elder man, confusion may set in as he prepares to die. This is transition time, and transitions always breed confusion.

Transition
Transition time means that there are no pure stages on this journey. No man is purely phallic, warrior, or sage. The lust of *zakar*, the fire of *gibbor*, the wound of *enosh*, the maturity of *'ish*, the wisdom of *zaken*—each is a part of me every day, though we transition from one stage to another.

Separation
When a man recognizes he is still a phallic kind of guy, it forces him to deal with the phallic issues in his life; only then can he move on and grow up a little. This means saying goodbye to the phallic stage. So it is with every stage. Without separation it is easy to make any one stop a permanent home, put down roots, and live there forever. That would be a tragedy, because there is so much more to the masculine journey.

Initiation
We as men have lost all of our formal initiation rites. In their absence, the peer group usually substitutes negative ones: smoking one's first cigarette, getting drunk, or bedding a girl. Adult ones are even more obscure or perverted: "Real men make money, play around, kill animals, cheat on their taxes," etc. Let's at least begin thinking about which appropriate initiation rites might fit each of these stages.

In a sense, our birthday is our first initiation rite to the *'adam* stage. Having my appendix taken out when I was nine was my first graphic experience of feeling my own mortality. Photos record the event.

Instead of jumping all over teenagers when they have their first experience with the police, alcohol, sex, or drugs, we could look on this as a teachable moment and a rite of passage. Perhaps the true elders could come forward and confess their own adolescent sins, and congratulate the next generation for being human. Then they could move on to the all-important issues of forgiveness and restoration, but on common ground with the young person, as a fellow sinner!

Traditionally, the initiation rite for the warrior has been the first kill. Athletic competitions award trophies; companies give bonuses to new employees who bag their first sales trophy. Yet I wonder how we might find appropriate ways of rewarding the spiritual-warrior.

If ever we needed to initiate the wounded male, it is now. A man's divorce, job firing, major health problem, legal battle, or sexual indiscretion, is a wound we show deference to as a part of the male journey. Instead of burying the wound or denying its pain, we need to see these experiences as potentially significant maturing events.

For the mature man, we must learn to celebrate launching out on a new career or seeking important family reconciliation. We might even consider celebrating the release of old illusions.

For the sage, many initiation components are already built into the physical body. Graying hair, going bald, wearing glasses, and retirement are humorously talked about. Retirement parties are common. But the intent is usually focused on all the wrong things. In the church we could celebrate anyone who is willing to take a risk at this late stage of life, start a new business, run for office, or take on a new ministry.

A Mentor Keeps Us Moving

Wherever I am on the masculine journey, I need a mentor who is at least one stage ahead of me, I need this to provide a model of masculinity and give the encouragement I need. It seems I haven't found those who were mature, honest, and self-confident enough that I could genuinely trust them with my inner life. I feel the vacuum significantly. But this is what we need God for.

Jesus as the Voice of God

Jesus is the One who moves us on from one stage to the next. He is the only One who can genuinely empathize with where we are, because He also has experienced the same stages on the masculine journey (Hebrews 4:15). Jesus as the second Adam (Romans 5:14) was very much human, He experienced the full range of human emotional and physical life, yet did not sin. Jesus was phallic with all the inherent phallic passions we experience as men. He was tempted in *every* way as we are without giving in.

Christ was the Warrior from day one of His career as

Messiah. For the sake of sinners, outcasts, women, children; for truth, compassion, justice; and for His Father's will. His actions as a warrior probably got Him crucified (Matthew 21:12,45).

For men who are experiencing woundedness, Jesus again is our model. As *the* Wounded Male, He struggled with obedience to His Father's will and betrayal by His disciples. With the Crucifixion, His wounding was complete. He was broken, bruised, bleeding, and dying (Luke 22:39–23:25).

In the resurrection, we see Jesus as *the* Mature Man, reconnecting with His disciples, encouraging them in their disillusionment (24:13-49), and bringing about reconciliation (John 21:1-25). The Risen Lord is the Ruler of life capable of bringing about restoration in the worst of our situations.

Jesus is also our Sage. He invested Himself in mentoring the men who would carry on the Kingdom work after He departed this earth (John 14:18, 16:7-15, 21:17). He is our sage, mentor, and continuous contributor to our lives. He is the voice we need at every stage on the masculine journey.

New Expressions of Faith at Every Stage
Rather than going through different developmental stages as in cognitive or moral development, faith is uniquely required at each point of our developmental journey. Faith is always day by day, event by event, and stage by stage. I wish I could reach a certain level of faith and then stay there, but this has not been my experience, nor do I believe this is biblical. At every point on the journey—with my phallic nature, with the wars I fight, with the wounds I suffer, with my vision and fears of the future—I face some unique area that demands a new expression of faith.

EXPLORING THE ISSUES WITH OTHER MEN

> **Note to the leader:** Rearrange the furniture in the room to correspond to places on the map on page 84 for use with the following questions. Label the location of each "city" around the room.

1. On the map on page 84, we have translated the metaphors of the masculine journey into humorous place names. Guided by the questions that follow, find yourself on the

map and write the specified initials. (You will probably mark four different cities, but if the same city applies more than once, you can mark it accordingly.)

◆ Which city have you only *passed through*? Write PT at that point.
◆ Where have you *stayed the longest*? Write SL at that city.
◆ Which place seems *most remote* to you? Write MR at that juncture.
◆ Which point do you want to *visit again*? Write VA there.

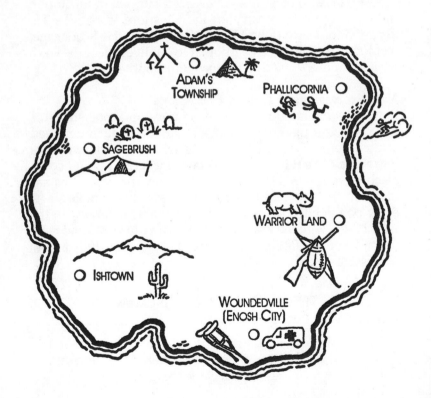

Your group leader will have arranged your meeting room to correspond to the map. Proceed to one of the places you initialed. If most men choose the same city, talk among yourselves to work out if some will go elsewhere. If no one else is at the city you choose, move to another city you initialed. The goal is to have pairs of men at cities relevant to each of them.

2. In your respective cities you will find a fellow struggler wrestling with the same issues as you are. Talk with that partner about the specific requirements of faith God is asking of you at that stage. Use these guidelines to start your ten-minute conversation:

   ◆ Creational men: talk about noble aspirations, unfulfilled expectations.
   ◆ Phallic men: talk about anxieties; e.g., a waxing or waning sex drive.
   ◆ Warriors: talk about your gun collection or latest sword fight.
   ◆ Wounded men: talk through your very real hurts, but don't whine.
   ◆ Mature men: talk about what you'll do with the rest of your life.
   ◆ Sages: talk about what you'll be remembered for, who you'll mentor.

3. Move around the room/map to a different city you initialed. Mix things up so that each man is with a new partner. Some men may have to remain in their original city to make the pairs work out. With your new comrade, have a ten-minute discussion on such questions as:

   ◆ How does a warrior need a wounded male mentor?
   ◆ How does a phallic man need a warrior?
   ◆ How does a wounded male need a mature man?
   ◆ How does a man keep from getting stuck at any one particular stage?

4. If you have more time, say goodbye to the city you are camped at, and rotate once more. This time don't worry about the places you initialed; just find a new partner. Discuss these questions:

85

- What kind of mentor do you need at your current stage in life?
- What kind of mentor can you be to a younger man?
- What options do you have if you cannot find someone who is mature, honest, self-confident to help you through the next step on your male journey?

PROFILING A BIBLE CHARACTER

Many men ask, "Where does Jesus fit into all this?" Robert Hicks answers, "He fits in very nicely," then concludes *The Masculine Journey* by telling you exactly how. The man Jesus is one of us at all the stages of a man's life. Therefore, Jesus is the Representative Man, the Ultimate Male Model, and the final Bible character we profile.

Note to the leader: You could assign each man one or two texts from question 5 and ask them to report their findings. Your goal is to get a composite picture and feeling for what Jesus went through.

---

5. Suppose you were to build a case study from Scripture to support Hicks' thesis: *The man Jesus is one of us at all the stages of a man's life.* What points along the masculine journey do you find Jesus going through, or identifying with, as you consider the following passages?

   Luke 3:23-38

   Luke 4:1-13

   Luke 4:16-30

   Luke 5:1-11

Luke 13:31-35

Luke 19:45-48

Luke 20:41-47

Luke 22:39-46

Luke 22:54-62

Luke 22:63-65

Luke 23:26-43

Luke 24:13-49

7. Put in the language of the masculine journey, Jesus was phallic, with all the phallic passions we as men experience. Jesus knew every temptation of the flesh yet did not sin. It follows logically that He was tempted in all ways sexually.

In what specific areas do you think Jesus was tempted? Which temptation of Jesus touches a felt need of yours, such that you could begin your walk with Him, or your talk with Him, at that point on the masculine journey? To help answer that question, see the profile of Jesus in Hebrews.

Hebrews 1:1-4

Hebrews 2:5-9

Hebrews 2:14-18

Hebrews 4:14-16

BRINGING IT HOME TO YOURSELF AND OTHER MEN

8. Jesus can be found at every stage of the masculine journey: one step ahead of you, to show you the way; side by side with you, to give you a shoulder to cry on. He can be trusted as our guide, but we still must place our faith in Him at every point. Pray with one other man, bringing to Christ your brother and bringing your brother to Christ. Consider the following suggestions for prayer:

   ◆ Phallic men: trust Christ with your sexuality, whether young or old, single or married, whether homosexually or heterosexually tempted.
   ◆ Warriors: trust Christ with the wars you choose to fight; agree not to shed innocent blood; learn from Him how to fight ethically.
   ◆ Wounded males: trust Christ with your wounds (from divorce, job loss, child's death); let Him give you hope and draw you out of your cave.
   ◆ Mature men: trust Christ to renew your (dulled) vision and reconcile all your (estranged) relationships; trust Him with the rest of your life.
   ◆ Elder sages: trust Christ with your fears and inevitable losses; leave your life's work to others; allow Christ to multiply the blessings.

9. Awards Night: The time has come to celebrate the growth within each man and your progress along the masculine journey (if for no other reason than you finished the study!). Think through the transitional events and defining moments of the "normative masculine journey" that *The Masculine Journey* mentions. Add to this list from

your own experience. Find appropriate awards and recognition that your men's group could do for one another, not only right now but whenever appropriate along the continuing male journey. This may begin as nothing more than a token gesture. Add to the suggestions listed here. Choose to do one or more right now, or make an appointment with another man to make your award presentation this week.

- ❑ Make an award certificate named for a Bible character embodying one trait.
- ❑ Congratulate a man for being human, while emphasizing forgiveness and restoration.
- ❑ Affirm an aspect of a man's warrior nature, sharpening his dull sword as "iron sharpens iron" (Proverbs 27:17).
- ❑ Give a "Purple Heart for Broken Spirits."
- ❑ Renew and channel someone's flagging energy by issuing a call to ministry.
- ❑ Write a letter to a friend, affirming the attributes you appreciate about him.
- ❑ Bequeath to someone your cherished mantle or trophy.
- ❑ Designate something special to a younger man in your last will and testament.
- ❑ Issue a recall of all Grecian Formula or Just for Men type products.

Note to the leader: You could prepare individual awards ahead of time to "knight" or "anoint" every man. Another approach to this Awards Night is an organized "strength bombardment" exercise, where each man takes a turn at center stage, while the others lay hands on him and pray affirmatively. Set aside extra time to conclude your journey together on a celebration note.

TAKING IT FURTHER WITH OTHER STUDIES

This last stop on the journey is really the first step on a new male journey. Many other men have gone before you, many more will come after you. If you have unanswered questions, review *The Masculine Journey* and its endnotes, which may spur you on to study the men's movement further. Look over the list of other NavPress study guides on page 96. Consider starting a group of your own.

If you want to study the Bible more on topics and characters related to the theme of *The Masculine Journey*, you could start by designing your own study around the life and times of the Apostle Paul. Drawing from the book of Acts and the epistles Paul wrote, he plainly exhibits all six male stages:

- ◆ Creational man—the "chief of all sinners" who knew firsthand about the noble savage within.
- ◆ Phallic man—urged men to "marry rather than burn with lust."
- ◆ Warrior—debated all comers, even the Roman authorities, "pummeled his body" and "fought the good fight."
- ◆ Wounded male—suffered great hardships at almost every stop along his journey.
- ◆ Mature man—built a network of Kingdom workers.
- ◆ Sage—mentored Timothy and "guards the gospel" as his last will and testament to the early church.

Help for Leaders

◆

This guide is ideal for a group of from four to twelve men. Because God has designed Christians to function as a body, we learn and grow more when we interact with others than we would on our own. If you are on your own, see if you can recruit a few men to join you in working through this guide. On the other hand, if you have a group larger than twelve you should divide into smaller groups of six or so for discussion. With more than twelve people, you begin to move into a large group dynamic, and not everyone has the opportunity to participate.

The main goal of the discussion leader is to guide the group in an edifying time centered on God's truth and grace. You may want one appointed man to lead all the sessions, or you may want to rotate leadership.

PREPARATION

Your aim as a leader is to create an environment that encourages participants to be honest with themselves, the group, and God. Group members should sense that no question is too dumb to ask, that the others will care about them no matter what they reveal about themselves, and that each person's opinion is as valid as everyone else's. At the same time, they should know that the Bible is your final authority for what is true.

As the group leader, your most important preparation for each session is prayer. You will want to make your prayers personal, of course, but here are some suggestions:

◆ Pray that group members will be able to attend the discussion consistently. Ask God to enable them to feel safe enough to share thoughts and feelings

honestly, and to contribute their unique gifts and
insights.
◆ Pray for group members' private times with God.
Ask God to be active in nurturing each man.
◆ Ask the Holy Spirit for guidance and insight in exer-
cising patience, acceptance, sensitivity, and wisdom.
Pray for an atmosphere of genuine caring in the
group, with each member being honestly open to
learning and change.
◆ Pray that your discussion will lead each of you to
obey the Lord more closely and demonstrate His
presence to others.

After prayer, your most important preparation is to be
thoroughly familiar with the material you will discuss. Before
each meeting, be sure to read the text and answer all of the
questions for yourself. This will prepare you to think ahead of
questions group members might raise.

Choose a time and place to meet that is consistent, comfortable, and relatively free from distractions.

LEADING THE GROUP

As you conduct each session keep the following in mind.

Work toward a safe, relaxed, and open atmosphere. This
may not come quickly, so as the leader you must model
acceptance, humility, openness to truth and change, and love.
Develop a genuine interest in each man's remarks, and expect
to learn from them. Listen carefully. Be affirming and sincere.

Pay attention to how you ask questions. By your tone of voice,
convey your interest and enthusiasm for the question and
your acceptance of the group members. They will adopt your
attitude.

If the discussion falters, keep these suggestions in mind:

◆ Be comfortable with silence. Let the group wrestle
to think of answers. Some of the questions require
thought or reflection. Don't be quick to jump in and
rescue the group with your answers.
◆ On the other hand, you should answer questions
yourself occasionally. In particular, be the first to
answer questions about personal experiences. In this

way you will model the depth you hope others will show. Count on this: If you are open, others will be too, and vice versa. Don't answer every question, but don't be a silent observer.

◆ Reword a question if you perceive that the group has trouble understanding it as written.

◆ If a question evokes little response, feel free to leave it and move on.

◆ When discussion is winding down on a question, go on to the next one. It's not necessary to push people to see every angle.

Ask only one question at a time. Often, participants' responses will suggest a follow-up question to you. Be discerning as to when you are following a fruitful train of thought and when you are going on a tangent.

Be aware of time. It's important to honor the commitment to end at a set time.

Encourage constructive controversy. The group members can learn a great deal from struggling with the many sides of an issue. If you aren't threatened when someone disagrees, the whole group will be more open and vulnerable. Intervene when necessary, making sure that people debate ideas and interpretations, not attack each others' feelings or character. If the group gets stuck in an irreconcilable argument, say something like, "We can agree to disagree here," and move on.

Encourage autonomy with the group members. With a beginning group, you may have to ask all the questions and do all the planning. But within a few meetings you should start delegating various leadership tasks. Help members learn to exercise their gifts. Let them make decisions and solve problems together. Encourage them to maturity and unity in Christ.

Validate both feelings and objective facts. Underneath the umbrella of Scripture, there is room for both. People's feelings are often a road map to a biblical truth they need, but truth takes time to sink in. Expressing feelings—even negative ones like anger and fear—helps a person become more able not to be controlled by them. Give group members permission to feel things they wouldn't feel if they totally understood and trusted God. But of course, participants are responsible to express feelings in ways that don't dominate the group or damage others.

Summarize the discussion. Summarizing what has been said

will help the group members see where the discussion is going and keep them more focused.

Don't feel compelled to "finish." It would be easy to spend an entire session on one or two questions. As leader, you will be responsible to decide when to cut off one discussion and move to another question, and when to let a discussion go on even though you won't have time for some questions. There will almost certainly be more questions than you need because we want you to be able to select those that seem most helpful for your unique group.

Let the group plan applications. The ideas in the section "Bringing It Home to Yourself and Other Men" are suggestions. Your group should adapt them to be relevant and life-changing for the members. If men see a genuine need that an application addresses, they are more likely to follow up. Help them see the connection between need and application.

End with refreshments. This gives members an excuse to stay for a few minutes and discuss the subject informally. Often the most important conversations occur after the formal session.

DURING THE FIRST SESSION

You or someone else in the group can open the session with a short prayer dedicating your time to God.

A discussion is much more productive and honest if the participants know each other. Some of the questions in the first session are designed to help participants get acquainted.

At some point during the session, go over the following guidelines. They will help make your discussion more fruitful.

Confidentiality. No one should repeat what someone shares in the group unless that man gives permission. Even then, discretion is imperative. Be trustworthy. Participants should talk about their own feelings and experiences, not those of others.

Attendance. Each session builds on previous ones, and you need continuity with each other. Ask group members to commit to attending all eight sessions unless an emergency arises.

Participation. This is a *group* discussion, not a lecture. It is important that each man participate in the group.

Honesty. Appropriate openness is a key to a good group. Be who you really are, not who you think you should be. On the other hand, don't reveal inappropriate details of your life simply for the shock value. The goal is relationship.

About Promise Keepers

◆

Promise Keepers is an organization dedicated to motivating men toward greater strength and Christlike masculinity.

Promise Keepers sponsors men's conferences in regional locations and various churches around the country. The annual Promise Keepers National Men's Conference is held each July in Boulder, Colorado.

Promise Keepers seeks to be a supply line to the local church, helping to encourage and assist pastors and ministry leaders in calling men to an accountable relationship with Jesus Christ and with one another. Promise Keepers wants to provide men's materials (like this guide) as well as seminars and the annual conference to emphasize the godly conviction, integrity, and action each of us needs.

Please join us in helping one another be the kind of men God wants us to be. Write or call our offices today.

Promise Keepers
P.O. Box 18376
Boulder, CO 80308

1-800-228-3100
or
1-303-421-2800

SMALL-GROUP MATERIALS FROM NAVPRESS

BIBLE STUDY SERIES

CRISISPOINTS FOR WOMEN
DESIGN FOR DISCIPLESHIP
GOD IN YOU
GOD'S DESIGN FOR THE FAMILY
INSTITUTE OF BIBLICAL
  COUNSELING SERIES

LIFECHANGE
LIFESTYLE SMALL GROUP SERIES
QUESTIONS WOMEN ASK
STUDIES IN CHRISTIAN LIVING
THINKING THROUGH DISCIPLESHIP

TOPICAL BIBLE STUDIES

Becoming a Woman of
  Excellence
Becoming a Woman of Freedom
The Blessing Study Guide
Caring Without Wearing
Celebrating Life
Crystal Clear
The Gift of Creation
Growing in Christ
Growing Strong in God's Family

Homemaking
Intimacy with God
Loving Your Husband
Loving Your Wife
A Mother's Legacy
Surviving Life in the Fast Lane
To Run and Not Grow Tired
To Walk and Not Grow Weary
What God Does When Men Pray
When the Squeeze Is On

BIBLE STUDIES WITH COMPANION BOOKS

Bold Love
From Bondage to Bonding
Hiding from Love
Inside Out
The Practice of Godliness
The Pursuit of Holiness
Secret Longings of the
  Heart

Transforming Grace
Trusting God
What Makes a Man?
The Wounded Heart
Your Work Matters to God

RESOURCES

Curriculum Resource Guide
How to Lead Small Groups
Jesus Cares for Women
The Small Group Leaders
  Training Course

Topical Memory System (KJV/NIV
  and NASB/NKJV)
Topical Memory System: Life
  Issues (KJV/NIV and
  NASB/NKJV)

VIDEO PACKAGES

Abortion
Bold Love
Hope Has Its Reasons
Inside Out

Living Proof
Parenting Adolescents
Unlocking Your Sixth Suitcase
Your Home, A Lighthouse